Wild Birds

ACROSS

The Prairies

Wild Birds

ACROSS

The Prairies

TEXT AND PHOTOGRAPHY
BY WAYNE LYNCH

ASSISTED BY AUBREY LANG

FIFTH
HOUSE
PUBLISHERS

Front cover image (avocet) by Wayne Lynch
Back cover images (sage grouse and burrowing owl) by Wayne Lynch
Cover and interior design by John Luckhurst / GDL

We acknowledge the support of
The Canada Council for the Arts for our publishing program.

THE CANADA COUNCIL | LE CONSEIL DES ARTS
FOR THE ARTS | DU CANADA
SINCE 1957 | DEPUIS 1957

We acknowledge the financial support of the Government of Canada through the
Book Publishing Industry Development Program for our publishing activities.

Printed in Canada.

99 00 01 02 03 / 5 4 3 2 1

CANADIAN CATALOGUING IN PUBLICATION DATA

Lynch, Wayne
    Wild birds across the prairies
    ISBN 1-894004-21-3
        1. Birds—Prairie Provinces—Identification. 2. Birds—Prairie Provinces—Pictorial Works. I. Title.
    QL685.5.P7L96 1999   598'.09712   C98-911155-5

Published in Canada by   Published in the U.S. by
Fifth House Ltd.   Fitzhenry & Whiteside
#9 - 6125 11 St. SE   121 Harvard Avenue
Calgary, AB, Canada   Suite 2
T2H 2L6   Allston, Massachusetts
                                02134

Contents

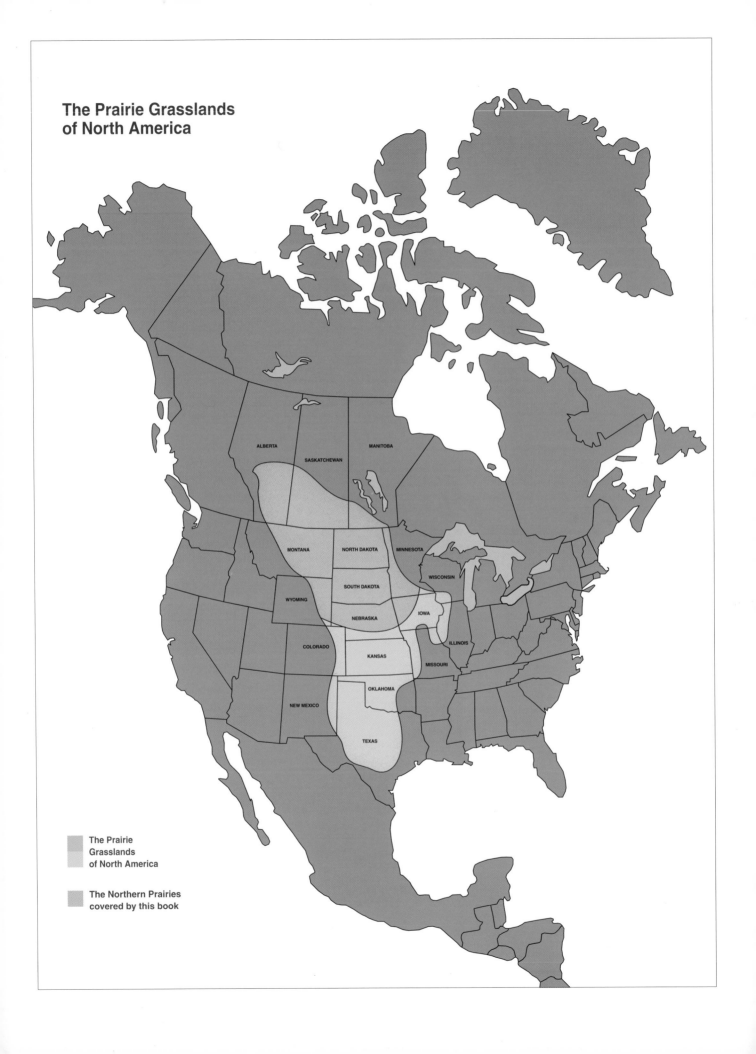

The Prairie Grasslands
of North America

ALBERTA
SASKATCHEWAN
MANITOBA
MONTANA
NORTH DAKOTA
MINNESOTA
WISCONSIN
SOUTH DAKOTA
WYOMING
NEBRASKA
IOWA
ILLINOIS
COLORADO
KANSAS
MISSOURI
OKLAHOMA
NEW MEXICO
TEXAS

The Prairie
Grasslands
of North America

The Northern Prairies
covered by this book

Introduction

It was a bitterly cold April morning. I had slept in the open under a crystalline prairie sky, and a rim of frost glittered on the sagebrush near my head. I could hear the familiar plop and gurgle of sage grouse calling on their dancing grounds just 20 meters (65 ft.) away. Barely awake and reluctant to leave the warmth and comfort of my sleeping bag, I crept slowly on my hands and knees to my photo blind. It was 5:15 AM. I shivered and waited in the dark so the birds would be accustomed to me by the time dawn broke. After an hour and a half, the sun finally cracked the horizon, flooding the prairie with amber light and highlighting the feathered beauty of the two dozen magnificent sage grouse that surrounded my blind. For the next two hours I watched them strut their stuff, fight, chase, and mate. Witnessing this wildlife spectacle was enough reward; it mattered little if I captured the moment on film. As had happened so often before, I was mesmerized by the natural wonder of birds.

I became enchanted by the prairie grasslands more than 20 years ago and have been bewitched by birds even longer. This book combines both of these personal passions. But it is more than a book about birds of the prairies; it is a celebration of the beauty and biology of the natural world. Originally, native prairie grasslands occupied the entire central core of North America. This vast expanse of grass and sky stretched from the northern coniferous forests of Canada south to Texas, and from the jagged summits of the Rocky Mountains to the eastern hardwood forests. Today, 80 percent of the continent's grasslands are no more than a memory, and native prairie continues to disappear at a rate of 40,000 hectares (100,000 acres) a year. It is no surprise that grassland birds are declining more rapidly than any other avian community in North America. The best way to preserve these last remnants of prairie grasslands and their wildlife is to understand what we will lose if we do nothing to protect them. Grassland birds live complex and intriguing lives, and in *Wild Birds Across the Prairies* I share with you the many fascinating details that make these creatures so interesting and satisfying to watch.

Roughly 350 species of birds are found in the

A pair of sculpted sandstone hoodoos stands sentry over the arid badlands of Alberta's Dinosaur Provincial Park.

1

One-third of prairie sloughs, such as this one in North Dakota, dry up by mid-July.

Stands of sage-brush provide important summer nesting habitat and critical winter feeding areas for sage grouse.

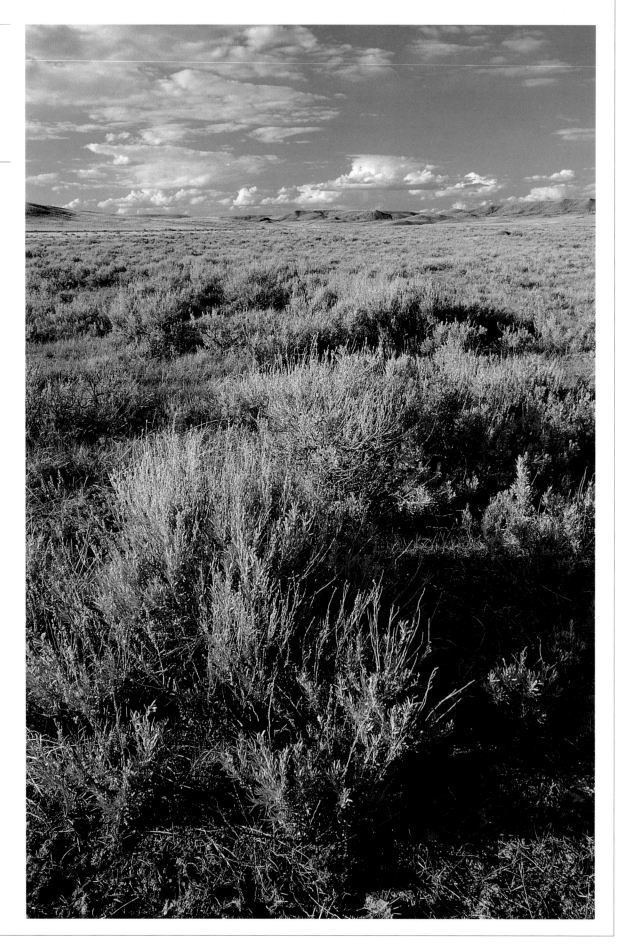

prairies of Canada and the northern United States. They can be divided into four convenient categories. The first group, which accounts for about 15 percent of the total, is the year-round residents, including such familiar birds as grouse and some owls. Seasonal breeders that move to the prairies for the spring and summer are the largest group; roughly half of all prairie birds fall into this category. A third group, the migrants, passes through the prairies in the spring and autumn en route to and from the boreal forest or the Arctic. This group consists mainly of shorebirds, waterfowl, and wood warblers and makes up about a quarter of the total bird population. The winter visitors are the smallest group—10 percent of all prairie birds—and include such favorites as birds of prey, finches, and some Arctic owls. To provide as much diversity as possible, I have included birds from all four categories. I also selected birds that are relatively easy to find and those with which I have had considerable field experience. In addition, I included birds that have been studied well; research has revealed fascinating details of their biology.

Another way I tried to make the book more diverse was to choose birds from a variety of prairie habitats. The habitat that most people associate with the prairies is the rolling grassy plains. Yet the prairie grasslands is a wonderful and surprising mosaic of many habitats. It includes wetlands, such as sloughs and marshes, rimmed with waving stands of cattails, as well as lazy, winding rivers and large alkaline lakes. It also contains rolling dunescapes, sculpted badlands of multicolored sandstone, and inviting wooded river valleys and coulees where you can retreat from the glare of the open skies. Together, these different wild habitats combine to make the prairie grasslands, and the birds that fill its skies, a natural sanctuary to soothe the psyche, challenge the mind, and rekindle the spirit.

Aspens grow in the shelter of many prairie coulees where they are somewhat protected from dry prairie winds.

Wild Birds Across the Prairies

Red-necked Grebe

Podiceps grisegena

Family Details

Grebe Family, 22 species worldwide, 6 prairie species

Grebes are a common group of water birds found on sloughs and lakes across the prairies. Although they resemble ducks in size, grebes have a slender, pointed bill, not a flat one as most ducks have. Grebes are superb divers. The position of their legs at the back of their bodies gives them power and maneuverability in the water. Because their legs are so far to the rear, they walk with difficulty, and it is almost impossible for them to take off from land. Takeoff from the water, however, is not much better. All grebes have relatively small wings for their body size, so they must patter across the surface of the water for quite a distance before they can gain enough speed to become airborne. When swimming, these attractive water birds have the uncanny ability to disappear underwater without a ripple, and the speed with which they can do this has earned them several colorful nicknames: "devil-diver," "hell-diver," and "water witch."

Field Identification

The red-necked grebe has a stout, yellow bill, a long, chestnut-colored neck, white throat and cheeks, and black forehead and cap. Male and female plumage is almost identical.

Where to Find

This grebe is usually found on lakes and larger sloughs with cattails or bulrushes bordering the shoreline.

This male red-necked grebe is swimming towards the family nest, which is floating among nearby reeds.

Wintering Grounds

It spends the winter on salt water along the Atlantic and Pacific coasts of the continent.

Diet and Feeding Habits

The red-neck makes dives that last between 20 and 40 seconds. It feeds near the bottom on small fish, aquatic insects, tadpoles, and tiger salamanders.

Breeding Biology

The red-necked grebe, in common with other family members, are loudmouth lovers. Courting pairs swim side by side, their crests raised, and together sing an entertaining duet that sounds like a loud horse whinny. Typically, a nesting pair defends a territory of about 4 hectares (10 acres), so large lakes and sloughs may contain several pairs of these noisy grebes. In May and June, the birds build a floating nest of aquatic vegetation, which they anchor to cattails or rushes in water about a meter (3 ft.) deep. A clutch of three to six blue-white eggs is incubated for about three weeks, and both sexes share in the nest duties. The downy chicks leave the nest soon after they hatch, and although they can swim right away they spend the first three weeks of life riding on their parents' backs.

Eared Grebe

Podiceps nigricollis

Family Details

Grebe Family, 22 species worldwide, 6 prairie species

See Red-necked Grebe for a general discussion of the Grebe Family.

Field Identification

The eared grebe has bright red eyes, a slightly upturned, thin, black bill, rusty sides, and a black head and neck adorned with a pair of distinctive golden "ear" tufts. The female's coloration, especially her golden ear tufts, is slightly duller than the male's.

Where to Find

Eared grebes are gregarious in all seasons and prefer large sloughs and lakes with enough open water to support multiple pairs of breeding birds.

Wintering Grounds

They sometimes winter inland in Nevada, New Mexico, and Utah but are more common along the Pacific and Atlantic coasts of North America.

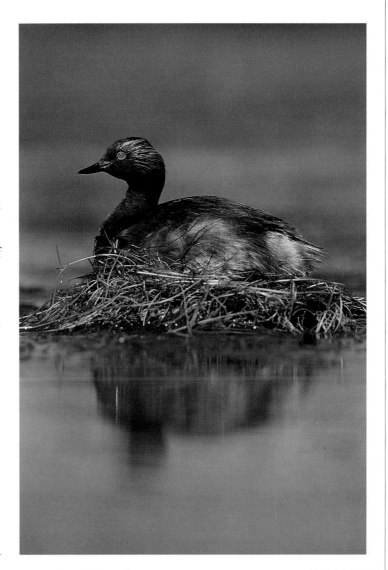

Diet and Feeding Habits

The bird feeds on leeches, dragonfly larvae, diving beetles, molluscs, small fish, and amphibians. Lobed toes, characteristic of all grebes, enable the bird to propel itself to depths of 7 meters (23 ft.), although it more commonly forages in shallow water.

Breeding Biology

The eared grebe frequently breeds in large colonies, sometimes containing several thousand pairs. The nest is a mound of green and rotting vegetation floating in water as shallow as 10 centimeters (4 in.), but I have flooded my chest waders often enough pursuing photographs of these handsome grebes to know that they regularly nest in much deeper water. Many years ago I photographed a dense colony of eared grebes in Wascana Park in the center of Regina, Saskatchewan. Most of the nests were 3 or 4 meters (10–13 ft.) apart, but in a few cases they almost touched one another.

Eared grebes lay three to five chalky, bluish white eggs that soon become stained brown. Whenever a parent leaves the eggs, it covers them with rotting

Spring windstorms can produce waves large enough to swamp the floating nest of an eared grebe.

nesting material to hide them from the sharp eyes of predators such as crows and gulls. Thus the pale eggs quickly turn brown. In *The Birds of Alberta*, Ray and Jim Salt mused: "It is surprising that anything could hatch in such a sodden mess, but after about three weeks, gray and white fluffy youngsters, all neck and legs, peer out from under the parent at the watery world around them." The chicks leave the nest within a day of hatching and immediately climb onto a parent's back, where they can snuggle under a wing to shelter themselves from cold spring downpours, hail, and the heat of the sun. The small grebelets commonly stay aboard the parent's back even when the adult dives underwater to search for food. In mild weather, the chicks ride with their heads poking out.

Trivia Tidbits
Young grebes are the original skinheads, and they have a novel way of communicating with their parents. The boldly striped youngsters have a triangular patch of bare skin on the top of their head that flushes deep red when they get excited, especially when begging for food. Scientists speculate the parents may use the color of the skin to monitor a chick's hunger.

Horned Grebe
Podiceps auritus

Family Details
Grebe Family, 22 species worldwide, 6 prairie species
See Red-necked Grebe for a general discussion of the Grebe Family.

Field Identification
This medium-sized grebe has bright crimson eyes, a straight, black bill tipped with white, rusty sides and neck, and a black head with golden "horns." The female's plumage is slightly duller than the male's. The horned grebe can be easily confused with the eared grebe. The neck color of the two birds is the easiest way to distinguish between them.

Where to Find
The horned grebe tends to select sloughs of open water that are fairly small, often less than 1 hectare (2.5 acres) in size.

Wintering Grounds
This small, handsome waterbird winters along the Atlantic and Pacific coasts of North America, within sight of the shore.

This handsome pair of horned grebes is engaged in a courtship display called the "penguin dance."

A pair of horned grebes may build a nest in just three hours, but add more material later.

Diet and Feeding Habits

It may feed on the surface, taking water striders, back swimmers, and mosquito larvae, but more often the horned grebe dives for its meals and hunts small fish, tadpoles, leeches, and other aquatic invertebrates. During these dives, the grebe may stay submerged for up to three minutes and travel more than 150 meters (490 ft.) underwater. With such underwater endurance these birds sometimes seem to disappear.

Breeding Biology

The horned grebe is usually a solitary nester, but four or five pairs may form a loose colony on larger lakes and marshes. Courtship includes a "weed dance," in which the partners, each with a beak full of soggy weeds, rush side by side across the water's surface. Head-shaking and bill-touching displays complete the ceremony.

The nest consists of a water-logged platform of floating weeds usually surrounded by a few stems of cattails or bulrushes. Strong prairie winds can whip up sizeable waves on the surface of a slough, and without the protection of above-water vegetation a grebe nest would soon be swamped. The pair never retrieves eggs that are washed out of a nest during a storm. The four to five nest-stained eggs hatch after 24 days. For the first month or so, the chicks eat, sleep, and travel on a parent's back. As they grow, they paddle behind the weary adults, incessantly begging to be fed, as all offspring seem to do. The free lunches stop when the young grebes are about two months old and have begun to fly.

Trivia Tidbit

The waterproof plumage on a grebe is especially soft and thick, and it may have over 20,000 feathers on its body. In the late 1800s, grebes were heavily hunted, and their thick feathers were marketed as "grebe fur" and used to adorn the capes and hats of stylish women of the era. Long before the grebe furriers came along, however, the grebes were using their feathers in a way that is unique among birds. Grebes pluck and eat their own feathers on a regular basis. Over half the contents of a horned grebe's stomach may consist of feathers. Researchers speculate that the feathers may line the grebe's stomach and protect it from sharp fish bones. Another possibility is that the feathers may filter sharp food debris and prevent it from entering the intestine. The wad of feathers, bones, and debris is then regurgitated and spit out as a harmless pellet. No matter why grebes feast on feathers, the behavior is crucial to them. Day-old grebe chicks are fed small feathers by their parents, sometimes even before they are given any food!

Pied-billed Grebe
Podilymbus podiceps

Family Details

Grebe Family, 22 species worldwide, 6 prairie species

See Red-necked Grebe for a general discussion of the Grebe Family.

Field Identification

The pied-billed grebe is the smallest and most secretive of the prairie grebes. The surest way to identify this small grebe is by its beak. The bird has a bluish white henlike beak, with a black band around it. Notwithstanding its all-brown coloration and black throat, the pied-billed grebe is anything but plain-looking.

Where to Find

The pied-bill likes dense stands of cattails and bulrushes and frequently settles on sloughs and small ponds with relatively little open water. In this way, it differs from other prairie grebes, which prefer less vegetation and more open water.

Wintering Grounds

The pied-bill migrates in small numbers at night, as do all grebes, and most have left the prairies by the end of October. The majority migrates to inland lakes and marshes in the southern United States, although some grebes winter on salt water along the southern coast of the country.

Diet and Feeding Habits

Last spring I watched an ambitious pied-bill try to swallow a large leopard frog. The bird repeatedly shook the frog, dropped it in the water, and picked it up again. After several minutes of such "tenderizing" the grebe was still unable to dismember or swallow its catch. The bird swam behind some cattails before I saw how the meal ended. Pied-billed grebes normally tackle much smaller prey than frogs. They hunt in shallow water for small fish, aquatic beetles, bugs, leeches, and the larvae of midges, dragonflies, and damselflies. When hunting, they usually stay submerged for less than 10 seconds.

Breeding Biology

The pied-bill is heard far more often than it is seen. The male's territorial song is a loud, throaty *kow, kow, kow,* which can be heard up to a kilometer (0.5 mi.) away. The loud call penetrates the thick stands of cattails and rushes in which these birds live, and their courtship consists mainly of vocal displays.

The elaborate visual displays used by the other prairie grebes in open water would be much less effective in the confusion of stems and leaves where pied-bills prefer to live.

Pairs build a soggy platform nest of vegetation in shallow water. I have often looked for their nests and can attest to how well hidden they are among the cat-tails. In many cases, the birds will build two nests, but use only the second one to cradle their eggs. The first nest is used for loafing and copulation. Pied-bills lay four to seven plain, whitish eggs and both partners share in the three-week incubation. The adults care for the chicks for one more month, by which time the young grebes are hunting for themselves and making their first clumsy flights.

Trivia Tidbit
Daily feather care, called preening, is necessary for all birds, especially water birds such as grebes. A mixture of fat, wax, and water is produced by a nipple-shaped preen gland located on the bird's lower back at the base of its tail. The bird squeezes out the waxy secretion with its beak and methodically spreads it over its feathers. Biologists believe the secretion helps in a number of ways. It makes feathers waterproof, discourages feather lice, and its antifungal and antibacterial properties protect the bird's plumage from damaging microorganisms. Likely the secretion also keeps a bird's beak and legs from drying out.

This pied-billed grebe is about to regurgitate a compact pellet of indigestible food remains, a common behavior in grebes.

American White Pelican

Pelecanus erythrorhynchos

Family Details

Pelican Family, 7 species worldwide, 1 prairie species

Pelicans are hard to confuse with any other water bird. They are massive birds with a wingspan reaching nearly 3 meters (10 ft.); some individuals may weigh as much as 13.5 kilograms (30 lb.), making them among the heaviest of flying birds. Their large beak and pouch are distinctive and inspired the famous limerick by Dixon Lanier Merritt: "A marvellous bird is the pelican, his bill holds more than his belly can. He can hold in his beak, enough food for a week, and I wonder how the hell he can." A pelican's beak, in fact, can hold nearly 11 liters (3 gal.) of water, a hundred times the capacity of the human mouth.

The horny fin on the upper beak of male and female white pelicans drops off soon after egg laying is finished.

Field Identification

The pelican is a large, white bird with black wingtips visible only when the bird is in flight. The black on the wing is the surest way to distinguish the white pelican from the tundra swan, another large, white bird. Despite its size, the pelican is a graceful flier, and groups of them may soar high on the updrafts of warm mid-day thermals.

Where to Find

The white pelican prefers large lakes with secluded islands for nesting. The birds may use smaller lakes and sloughs for fishing and loafing.

Wintering Grounds

The bird winters in central California and along the Pacific coast as far south as Guatemala, and also along the shores of the Gulf of Mexico. The pelican returns to the prairies in early May.

Diet and Feeding Habits

The white pelican eats fish, mostly species ignored by human anglers, and catches them in shallow water, 0.3–2.5 meters (1–8 ft.) deep. They commonly fish in the open areas of sloughs and marshes, along lakeshores, and below rapids. They locate fish by sight during the day and by touch during the night. The white pelican frequently hunts in groups, a line of swimming birds driving the fish ahead of them. Over and over again (four to six times per minute) each bird dips its bill and scoops up a pouch full of water. The dipping tends to become more coordinated when they find fish. A pelican trying to swallow a large fish may be attacked by another pelican wanting to steal its meal. An adult bird consumes about 1.5 kilograms (3.3 lb.) of fish a day. The white pelican, unlike its relative the brown pelican, never dives for fish from the air.

Breeding Biology

The pelican nests in large colonies, up to several hundred pairs, on secluded islands free from predators such as red foxes and coyotes. Nesting colonies are extremely vulnerable to human disturbance, and a single visit early in the nesting season may cause an entire colony to desert.

Courtship includes "circle-flying," in which one or more pairs circle and soar above a nesting lake. The nest is a simple shallow depression on the ground sparsely lined with rocks, sticks, and rushes. In large colonies, the nests are usually spaced close together, typically just beyond the pecking distance of irritable neighbors. Beginning in June, two large, dull white eggs are incubated in shifts by both parents. After about 30 days, a pair of orange, naked, wrinkled, wobbly-necked "space aliens" crack their way into the world. The first chick usually hatches a day or two before its sibling and grows much faster. The second chick rarely survives, usually dying from starvation and continual pecking by its nestmate.

At around two and a half weeks the adults begin to leave their chicks unattended and the youngsters gather in pods, or crèches. Crèching may offer some protection from aerial predators such as large gulls, ravens, bald eagles, and great horned owls. Parents recognize the distinctive "whining grunt" of their own chick and feed only their own. Colonies are abandoned in late August and early September.

Trivia Tidbit

Twenty-five years ago, fewer than 16,000 breeding pairs of American white pelicans were left in the birds' nesting range in central North America. Today, there are more than 50,000 pairs, and the bird has been removed from the threatened-species list.

Double-crested Cormorant

Phalacrocorax auritus

Family Details

Cormorant Family, 39 species worldwide, 1 prairie species

The cormorants are a group of medium-sized diving birds with long, slim necks and slender, hooked beaks. On land, the birds often perch with their wings outstretched. The birds rest like this to dry their feathers, which become waterlogged after just a short time of swimming. The birds' soggy plumage probably makes them less buoyant, and as a result, they are able to dive more easily. Most people associate cormorants with the seaside, and they may seem out of place in the arid prairies. However, the prairie-nesting, double-crested cormorant is extremely adaptable and ranges throughout central North America as well as in the Caribbean and on the Pacific coast, from Alaska to Baja, Mexico.

Field Identification

The cormorant is a large, black bird with a long neck and tail, and a featherless, bright orange throat patch. In flight, the bird's neck is outstretched, unlike the heron, which hunches its head between its shoulders. When travelling in groups, cormorants fly silently in V-formation or in a line. The bird's most photogenic feature is its bright green eyes, which I think match the beauty of polished jade.

Where to Find

The cormorant prefers large rivers, sloughs, and lakes.

Wintering Grounds

It spends the cold winter months on coastal and inland waterways in the southeastern and southwestern United States.

Diet and Feeding Habits

The cormorant is an agile diving bird that feeds mainly on fish, but also eats crayfish, frogs, and salamanders. Cormorants, like grebes and loons, are foot-propelled divers that swim with powerful strokes of their large, webbed feet. Among prairie birds, cormorants are the deepest divers, reaching depths of 25 meters (82 ft.), although they usually hunt in much shallower water. When a cormorant catches a fish it brings it to the surface before

During a dive a cormorant's wing feathers become waterlogged, and the bird must dry them out afterwards.

day intervals, and the parents begin to incubate as soon as the first egg is laid. As a result, the first chick may be more than a week old when the last chick finally cracks loose. When fish are plentiful everyone in the family is fed, but when the meals are meagre the smallest chicks starve. Sometimes only one chick out of four may survive. Biologists call this behavior "facultative brood reduction." This simply means a cormorant pair starts out with the largest family it can possibly feed and the prevailing food conditions determine how many chicks survive.

Trivia Tidbit
The cormorant and the pelican incubate their eggs differently from all other prairie birds. Most birds have a small, featherless, vascularized area of skin on their belly called a "brood patch," which they use to warm their eggs. Cormorants and pelicans have no brood patch. Instead they use the large webs on their feet to cover their eggs and warm them. Breakage in cormorant eggs is rare, as they have especially thick shells.

Northern Pintail

Anas acuta

Family Details
Waterfowl Family,
147 species worldwide, 20 prairie species

Waterfowl, which include ducks, geese, and swans are a group of large, semi-aquatic birds, all of whom swim well and fly strongly. Waterfowl have a thick undercoat of down feathers, which the females pluck from their bodies to line and warm their nests. All young waterfowl are precocious when they hatch; their eyes are open, they are covered with fluffy down, and they are wound up for action. The young leave the nest almost immediately after hatching and follow their parents. From the beginning, the hatchlings feed themselves, although their parents may help them to locate food.

Prairie ducks can be divided into two broad categories: divers and dabblers. Watching how a particular duck feeds and how it takes flight will allow you to distinguish between the two groups. Dabblers either paddle along the top of the water, skimming food off the surface, or go bottoms up, stretching their necks underwater to reach food just below the surface. When dabblers take off, they jump straight into the air and are gone. This is the surest way to identify the dabbling group of ducks.

The diving ducks, as their name suggests, usually

swallowing it. This habit sometimes gets the cormorant into trouble. When they can, pelicans attack cormorants and steal their fish. I once saw a bald eagle swoop down on a fishing cormorant. The startled cormorant dropped its catch, and in the flash of a talon, the eagle flew off with the meal.

Breeding Biology
Their typically crowded colonies can be found on secluded islands in the middle of large sloughs and lakes. Less commonly, they also nest in the tops of dead trees. I have watched one ground-nesting colony in southeastern Alberta for almost 10 years. Fifty to 60 pairs nest on an island about 0.5 kilometers (0.3 mi.) from the shoreline. By late May in a typical year, the bulky nests of cattails, rushes, and sticks have been built, the eggs (three or four per nest) have been laid, and the first of the rubbernecked youngsters has hatched. Nothing is homelier than a wrinkled, featherless, black cormorant chick, and its lack of good looks is not the only strike against it. Cormorants lay their eggs at two- to three-

dive completely underwater when searching for food, and may remain submerged for up to a minute. These ducks have bigger feet than the dabblers, and their legs are positioned closer to the rear of their bodies, giving them more underwater power and steering ability. On land, however, the position of their legs produces an awkward gait. Diving ducks must take off from the water, running across the surface to build up speed before they become airborne.

Field Identification
The drake pintail is unmistakable. It sports a chocolate brown head and a long, slender, white neck with a thin, white line extending up behind its ear. Its sides and back are grayish, with black under its pointed tail. In flight, the trailing edge of its inner wing, called the speculum, is iridescent bronze-green edged with white. The female's plumage is a cryptic mottled brown.

Where to Find
The pintail is widespread throughout the prairies. The duck favors shallow sloughs and marshes, and semi-permanent wetlands, especially seasonally flooded fields.

Wintering Grounds
They winter along both continental coastlines and throughout the interior of Mexico and the southern United States.

Diet and Feeding Habits
Pintails are dabblers. During the breeding season, they eat mostly aquatic invertebrates: snails, crustaceans, fly larvae, water boatmen, and earthworms. They also dabble for seeds, especially those of grasses and bulrushes.

Breeding Biology
These elegant waterfowl are graceful, acrobatic fliers, and their courtship is a delight to watch. The males chase prospective mates in fast-wheeling "pursuit flights" that feature rapid dives from great heights and low, ground-hugging flight. These conspicuous aerial displays commonly involve two or three drakes following a single hen, but as many as 16 males may be in pursuit. The flights usually last less than four minutes, but the rare one may carry on for over half an hour. Pintails are among the earliest nesting ducks on the prairies. Writers Ray and Jim Salt, in *The Birds of Alberta*, summarized: "Before the end of April the female has concealed her nest in a meadow, under a

A trio of drake northern pintails dabbles for seeds on the bottom of a shallow prairie slough.

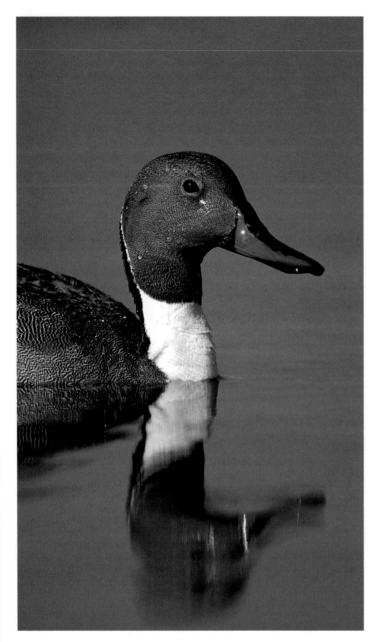

ducks sport a drabber mottled mix of browns, tans, and grays. In contrast, male and female geese have similar plumage. Whereas ducks eat fish, crustaceans, aquatic insects, and plant life, geese are primarily vegetarians, and though geese are accomplished swimmers they do not always feed in the water, and many spend considerable time foraging in fields for grain and greenery.

One very big difference between ducks and geese is the strength of the pair bond. All prairie ducks mate with a different partner each year, and the pair bond typically breaks down soon after the eggs are laid. The female duck is a single mother from that point on. In geese, however, the pair bond is very strong, often lasting a lifetime. During the nesting season, the male goose assumes an important role in family duties. He defends the territory from trespassers, he may help to incubate the eggs, he guards the female while she incubates, and he accompanies the goslings on outings and protects them from predators. In autumn, geese migrate as a family. The faithful pair stays with each other on the wintering grounds, and flies north together the following spring.

Mallard

Anas platyrhynchos

Family Details
Waterfowl Family, 147 species worldwide, 20 prairie species

See Northern Pintail for a general discussion of the Waterfowl Family.

Field Identification
The male mallard is the most familiar of all wild ducks. His metallic green head and neck, yellow bill, and chestnut breast make him hard to miss. In flight, his inner wings feature a violet patch bordered in front and behind by a strip of white. The female, like all prairie ducks, is a mottled brown.

Where to Find
The mallard is one of the most widespread and adaptable species of ducks. It occurs wherever there is fairly shallow water, either still or slowly flowing.

Wintering Grounds
This duck is extremely hardy, and it winters as far north as there is open water, including many locations in the southern Canadian prairies.

Male pintails migrate to the northern prairies in early April and are among the first ducks to return in spring.

bit of roadside brush, or in a cultivated field and is incubating her eggs when farm operations commence." Regrettably, thousands of pintail nests are accidentally destroyed during the routine burning and cultivation of stubble fields every spring.

The female alone incubates the clutch of seven to nine creamy yellow eggs and leads the ducklings to water when they hatch after 25 days. Pintails often build their nest far from water, and the downy ducklings may have to waddle 2 kilometers (1.2 mi.) or more to reach the safety of a slough or pond. The pintail family makes this dangerous journey at night when fewer predators are around.

Trivia Tidbits
Ducks and geese differ in a number of ways. Male ducks are typically brightly feathered, whereas female

Diet and Feeding Habits

The mallard dabbles for seeds, roots, and stems of grasses, pondweeds, sedges, and other aquatic vegetation. It also eats tadpoles, frogs, crustaceans, and insects. Young ducklings need fats and proteins for growth, and they eat mostly aquatic insects during the early weeks of their life.

Breeding Biology

Pairs form in the late fall on the wintering grounds. Courtship involves bill-dipping, head-flicking, and tail-shaking displays, with whistles, grunts, and quacks thrown in for auditory accompaniment. Throughout the winter, the drake protects the hen from the bothersome attention of rival males. This allows her to build up greater fat reserves, which she will need for migration and nesting. In spring, the drake follows the hen back to the nesting grounds, often to the same area where she herself was hatched and raised. As in most ducks, the drake abandons his mate soon after the eggs are laid, and the hen is left on her own to incubate the clutch and raise the ducklings.

With so many idle "divorced" drakes loafing around, it is not surprising that forced copulations have been reported in mallards, and many other species of waterfowl. Most of these aggressive attacks occur in the morning hours when eggs are most likely to be fertilized. Several males may attack at once, leaving the resident drake outnumbered and unable to defend his mate against them. Female mallards have even been killed during such "gang rapes."

Trivia Tidbit

The prairies are often called the "duck factory" of the continent, because more than half of all the ducks in North America are reared there. Eighty percent of all redheads, canvasbacks, pintails, and mallards start life on a prairie slough.

Thousands of years ago, in ancient China, the ubiquitous mallard was likely the first species of duck to be domesticated.

Prairie dabbling ducks can usually be identified by their voice; the male wigeon's is one of the most distinctive.

American Wigeon

Anas americana

Family Details

Waterfowl Family,
147 species worldwide, 20 prairie species

See Northern Pintail for a general discussion of the Waterfowl Family.

Field Identification

The wigeon is sometimes called the baldpate because of the conspicuous bright white crown on the male's head. This handsome drake also has an iridescent greenish patch on the sides of its head and sports rusty feathers on its sides. The female has a plain brownish body and a gray head. In flight, both sexes display a green speculum on their wings.

Where to Find

The wigeon is common on prairie ponds and sloughs.

Wintering Grounds

Most of these ducks migrate to the warmer climes of the extreme southern United States and farther south to the Caribbean and Central America.

Diet and Feeding Habits

The wigeon commonly dabbles in the shallow water and mud along the shoreline for the seeds and stems of grasses, sedges, rushes, and pondweeds. The wigeon is not a diving duck, but it still has a taste for many aquatic plants that are too deep for it to reach. The solution: piracy. I once watched a drake wigeon repeatedly attack an American coot every time it came to the surface with succulent plants it had torn loose from the bottom. Wigeons also bushwhack diving ducks such as canvasbacks and redheads and steal their meals.

Breeding Biology

Wigeons are among the earliest ducks to arrive on the prairies, returning in late April and early May, shortly after the pintails and mallards. The wigeon, like most ducks, begins to breed when it is one year old. Pairs form on the wintering grounds, and the drake follows the hen back to her chosen nesting area in the spring. Every season, the female has a different here-today-gone-tomorrow male partner, and she usually nests three or four times in her life. The hen, alone, builds a compact nest of grass and weeds, lined with down. Typically the nest is found near water. The ducklings usually hatch after three and a half weeks and fledge by the time they are six weeks old. Because they nest on the ground, the eggs of most prairie ducks are vulnerable to mammalian predators. Researchers in North Dakota found that 30 to 40 percent of wigeon nests were lost to keen-nosed mammals. As well, a five-year study in Alberta showed that four out of five wigeon nests were destroyed. In most cases, the egg-nappers were striped skunks.

Northern Shoveler

Anas clypeata

Family Details

Waterfowl Family, 147 species worldwide,
20 prairie species

See Northern Pintail for a general discussion of the Waterfowl Family.

Field Identification

The drake may sometimes be mistaken for a mallard since both ducks have a metallic green head. Other field signs to look for are a black "spoonbill," conspicuous yellow eye, bright white breast, and rusty-brown sides and belly. The brown cryptic coloration of the hen is similar to that of many prairie duck species, but her large orange-brown spoonbill is unique and relatively easy to spot.

Where to Find

Shovelers prefer shallow sloughs and marshes where there is submerged vegetation. These ducks often select wetlands with an equal mix of open water and cattails or rushes where they can hide.

Wintering Grounds

"Spoonies" winter on inland lakes and marshes throughout the southern United States and Mexico.

Diet and Feeding Habits

All prairie dabbling ducks have a comblike fringe along the edge of their upper and lower beak, which they use to strain food from the water. The birds draw mud and water into their mouths and then force it out through this filtering system. Of all the dabblers, the shoveler has the finest straining system. It feeds on a variable mix of seeds and aquatic invertebrates, sieved from the water, though it tends to eat more animal food than most dabblers do. Common foods include seed shrimps, snails, and copepods, many of which can occur in great numbers.

I'll never forget how I learned about the abundant invertebrate life that lurks in the bottom ooze of a prairie wetland. I wanted to photograph shovelers, so I set up a blind in the shallow water along the edge of a small slough. Because I had forgotten my hip waders, I stripped down to my underwear and went barefoot, enjoying the feel of the cool mud around my ankles and the squish of soft muck between my toes. I spent several hours cramped inside the blind, and only towards the end of my vigil did I get an inkling that I had made a mistake. The next day my lily-white feet were rosy-red, swollen, and covered with blistered, oozing bites. Nothing I did for days afterwards seemed to ease the itch. I swear to you, unkind critters live in prairie mud, so give a cheer for the filter-feeding dabblers.

Breeding Biology

The northern shoveler is one of the last dabblers to breed. In the Canadian prairies, peak nest-building for them occurs in the last week of May. The details of egg-laying and incubation in the shoveler follow the general pattern common to most dabblers. Typically, the hen lays an egg every day, and once the egg is laid, she covers it and leaves the nest for the rest of the day. She returns in the middle of the night, lays another egg in the early morning hours, and then leaves again for the day. Most shovelers lay 8 to 12 eggs in this way, and once the clutch is complete, the female does all the incubation. During the 25 days of incubation, the hen usually takes just two

The northern shoveler ranges well beyond the prairies of North America, occurring also in Europe, Asia, and Africa.

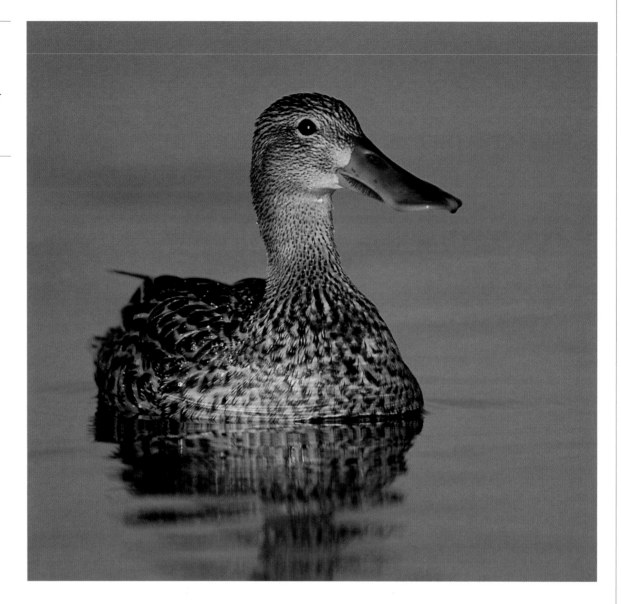

breaks a day, one in the morning and another in the afternoon. Each break lasts about an hour and a half and gives the female time to eat, drink, and preen.

Hatching is highly synchronized in shovelers, as it is in all waterfowl. The young begin to chirp while they are still inside the egg, several days before they hatch. Researchers speculate that this prehatching communication helps the ducklings to coordinate the timing of hatching. In shovelers, an entire clutch may hatch within four hours! Over the next seven weeks, the ducklings dabble, grow, and flap their way to independence.

Blue-winged Teal
Anas discors

Family Details
Waterfowl Family,
147 species worldwide, 20 prairie species
See Northern Pintail for a general discussion of the Waterfowl Family.

Field Identification
The blue-winged teal is one of the smallest prairie dabblers. With an average weight under half a kilogram (1 lb.), it takes three blue-winged teals to match the weight of a single mallard. The drake blue-wing is best identified by the distinctive white crescent on his dark blue face. In flight, the leading half of the duck's

inner wing is pale blue, although it can appear whitish in poor light. Female blue-wings are a mottled brownish gray, and their small size is one of the better clues to their identity.

Where to Find
Blue-wings are common on the prairies. They favor small, shallow ponds and sloughs, especially ones that have wet, grassy meadows nearby.

Wintering Grounds
These teals winter from the extreme southern United States, on through Mexico and Central America, to the northern countries of South America. One blue-wing that was banded in Delta Marsh, Manitoba, was later shot on a lake in Ecuador, 4000 meters (13,000 ft.) above sea level, on the slopes of Cotopaxi Volcano. The little teal had flown at least 6400 kilometers (3975 mi.) to reach its wintering grounds. Another hardy blue-wing, banded in Saskatchewan, flew to a marsh in Peru, a distance of at least 11,300 kilometers (7020 mi.). Apparently, blue-wings wintering in South America often migrate long distances over open water, an uncommon practise among dabbling ducks.

Diet and Feeding Habits
Three-quarters of the blue-winged teal's diet consists of the seeds of grasses and sedges, and the stems and leaves of pond weeds. The rest of the time it eats beetles, bugs, caddisfly larvae, the nymphs of damselflies and dragonflies, amphipods, seed shrimps, and snails.

Breeding Biology
Pairs usually form on the wintering grounds or during spring migration, so most of the blue-wings have a partner by the time they reach the prairies. From the time females arrive on the nesting grounds until they start to lay, they are feathered feeding machines, spending 50 to 70 percent of the day eating. There is a good reason for this: a clutch of teal eggs can equal 80 percent of the female's weight, so a great deal of energy is required to produce them. If a hen loses her clutch to predators, she may nest again, often choosing a site within 50 meters (164 ft.) of her earlier nest. These so-called "replacement clutches" are usually smaller—a reflection of the high energy drain imposed upon the female.

Like all dabblers, the drake blue-winged teal hangs around his mate just long enough to fertilize her and see her settled on the eggs, and then he leaves. The female incubates alone and stays with the ducklings for six to seven weeks until they finally fledge.

Trivia Tidbit
In mid-summer, all waterfowl become flightless for

Some prairie blue-wings migrate to northern South America, the farthest migration of any prairie duck.

several weeks while they molt and replace their flight feathers. The birds are especially vulnerable to predators at this time, and many of them flock together in open water on large lakes and sloughs for security. Some ducks, such as teals, stay hidden in cattails and bulrushes while they are molting, and come out to feed in the open only at night. Northern shovelers are particularly shy when molting and they stay hidden most of the time, feeding very little. As a result, they lose weight, but regain it quickly in a late summer feeding binge that fuels them for their migration south.

Cinnamon Teal

Anas cyanoptera

Family Details
Waterfowl Family, 147 species worldwide, 20 prairie species

See Northern Pintail for a general discussion of the Waterfowl Family.

Field Identification
The cinnamon teal is a fast flier that has been clocked at speeds of 80 kilometers per hour (50 mph). This teal is a small dabbler, only marginally larger than the blue-winged teal. The drake is unmistakable with his rich chestnut head and body, deep scarlet eyes, and powder blue patches on his inner wings. The drake cinnamon teal is the most beautiful duck on the prairies. The female, a cryptic mix of gray and brown, is difficult to distinguish from the female blue-wing, and when attempting identification it is probably best to admit defeat and immediately move on to another bird.

Where to Find
The cinnamon teal prefers marshes, flooded ditches, farm ponds, and the shallow margins of sloughs and lakes. It uses alkaline lakes more than most dabblers. In prairie Canada, the cinnamon teal is less widespread than most dabblers and is found mainly in southern Alberta and southwesten Saskatchewan.

Wintering Grounds
Many of these teals spend the winter in the southwestern United States, Mexico, and northern Central America, although some of them travel as far as northern South America.

Diet and Feeding Habits
In many areas, 80 percent of the cinnamon teal's diet consists of plants, mainly the seeds, leaves, and stems of rushes, sedges, grasses, and pondweeds. Some of these foods can be difficult to digest. The teal, in

The cinnamon teal usually feeds in shallow water and occasionally forages on dry land near the shore.

common with most waterfowl, has a muscular gizzard located midway between its mouth and its stomach. Here, seeds and other tough foods are ground up with the help of gravel and grit, which the birds swallow for this purpose. The gizzard of a bird serves the same function as the grinding molars of a mammal.

Breeding Biology

The courtship of the cinnamon teal takes place on the wintering grounds and includes chin-lifting, head-pumping, and pursuit flights. The pursuit flights usually involve a couple of chattering drakes chasing a solitary female. Cinnamon teal are extremely agile in flight, making sharp turns and fast, low-level passes. Shortly after a pair arrives on the spring breeding grounds, the male selects and defends a small territory of about 30 square meters (323 sq. ft.) or less. In most cases, the territory includes the nest site and a loafing area, which the drake uses while the hen is on the nest. In typical dabbler fashion, the drake cinnamon teal abandons his mate by the third week of incubation, and goes off to molt. The hen does all the incubation and cares for the ducklings.

A substantial portion of cinnamon teal nests, as many as a quarter of them, may be parasitized by other ducks. It is probably easy enough for another hen to sneak into a nest and lay an egg while the unsuspecting owner is away foraging. In a Utah study, redheads were the most common parasites, but other culprits included ruddy ducks, the northern shoveler, and the pintail. Cinnamon teals, however, are not always the victims; sometimes they are the offenders. Teals will parasitize the nests of others of their own kind, and will also occasionally leave an egg with an unwary mallard.

Trivia Tidbit

Until very recently, the waterfowl habit of eating gravel and grit caused the deaths of as many as three million ducks, geese, and swans every year. The cause: lead poisoning. For decades, the lead pellets from shotgun shells accumulated on the bottoms of prairie wetlands. For every duck killed by a hunter, it was estimated that 1400 pellets (almost a quarter of a kilogram or half a pound) settled on the bottom of a slough. The fine lead pellets were ingested incidentally when the birds were feeding, or were swallowed intentionally as grist for their gizzards. The lead from a single pellet was enough to poison a duck. In 1997, it finally became illegal to fire shotgun shells filled with lead pellets over any wetland or waterway.

Redhead and Canvasback

Aythya americana and *Aythya valisineria*

Family Details

Waterfowl Family, 147 species worldwide, 20 prairie species

See Northern Pintail for a general discussion of the Waterfowl Family.

The drake redhead acquires its full plumage splendor by the time it is one year old.

Field Identification

Both redheads and canvasbacks are diving ducks that submerge when feeding, and run across the water's surface to become airborne. The two divers have similar plumage: rusty heads, black chest, and whitish gray sides and back, and identification relies mainly on the head and bill shape, which are strikingly different. The canvasback has a long, sloping forehead and a large, all-black bill, whereas the redhead has a round head, a steep forehead, and a blue bill tipped with black. The females of both species are drabbly colored, with varying amounts of

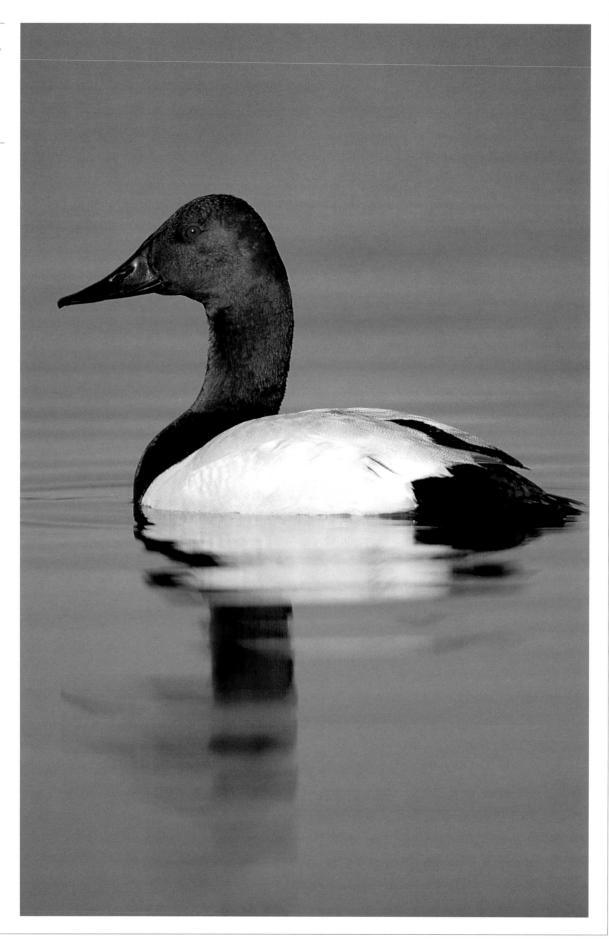

The male canvas-back, weighing up to 1.4 kilograms (3 lb.), is the heaviest diving duck on the prairies.

brown and gray. For both sexes, the characteristic head profile of the two ducks is usually enough to distinguish them. Once you acquire this kind of expertise, you can no longer consider yourself a casual duck watcher; you are a serious duckaholic.

Where to Find

Redheads and canvasbacks are common throughout the prairies. They are found on lakes, marshes, and sloughs, especially those bordered by bulrushes and cattails, which the ducks favor for nesting cover.

Wintering Grounds

The greatest numbers of these divers winter in sheltered coastal waters off California, and in the Gulf of Mexico. Hundreds of these ducks may gather in large offshore rafts to loaf, sleep, and feed.

Diet and Feeding Habits

Aquatic plants are the staple food of canvasbacks and redheads, though both ducks also feed on molluscs, midges, caddisflies, and other insects. When I first began to watch prairie ducks I wondered how so many species could share the same slough and not seriously compete with one another. The answer: habitat partitioning. By feeding in slightly different ways, in slightly different areas of the slough, and on slightly different foods, the various ducks lessen the competition among them. For example, the dabblers feed in the shallows and the divers in deeper water. The canvasback and redhead illustrate how subtle this partitioning can be. Both are diving ducks that commonly feed in open water up to 3 meters (10 ft.) deep, but when necessary, the slightly larger and heavier canvasback can dive to depths of 10 meters (33 ft.). The bill structure of the two ducks also differs. The redhead's beak is better designed to strain aquatic insects than is that of the canvasback, which is specialized for sieving plant foods. Finally, the two ducks commonly feed at different levels of the water column. Canvasbacks plunge to the bottom, tear out roots and tubers, and sieve the mud for seeds. Redheads, on the other hand, feed more on submerged stems and leaves from mid-water levels.

Breeding Biology

The basic breeding pattern is the same in diving ducks as it is in dabblers. Courtship and pairing occur on the wintering grounds or during spring migration. Once the birds arrive on the nesting grounds, the drake dutifully defends his mate from other males while she eats, eats, and eats, and then lays her eggs. His intentions, mind you, are totally selfish, as guarding the female is the best way to ensure his paternity. With the six to ten eggs laid, the drake promptly deserts his partner, and the hen is left to incubate the clutch by herself and care for the ducklings.

Canvasbacks and redheads, like all diving ducks, build their bulky reed nests over standing water, usually less than a meter (3 ft.) deep, and hide them in thick stands of cattails and bulrushes. This is quite different from the behavior of dabbling ducks, which typically nest on land, at times several kilometers from the nearest water. The main reason for the difference is anatomy. Dabblers walk well on land, and can take off from a jumping start, so it is easy for them to nest away from water. By doing so, they also have a large area in which to hide their nests from predators. Diving ducks, with their legs positioned farther back on their bodies, have difficulty walking on land and usually require a run across the water to become airborne. For both these reasons, they are tied to wetlands for nest sites.

Ruddy Duck

Oxyura jamaicensis

Family Details

Waterfowl Family,
147 species worldwide, 20 prairie species

See Northern Pintail for a general discussion of the Waterfowl Family.

Field Identification

The ruddy is a unique prairie duck belonging to a worldwide group of small diving ducks called "stiff-tails." The drake has a rusty neck and body, a black head with large white cheek patches, a sky blue bill, and a long, stiff tail that sometimes points straight upwards. Her stubby size and stiff tail best identify the brownish female. On takeoff, ruddy ducks patter across the water and beat their short wings so fast they are sometimes called "bumblebee ducks."

Where to Find

Ruddies are usually among the last prairie ducks to return in the spring. They are relatively common on marshes and sloughs, and they prefer wetlands that have a lot of vegetation poking above the water. Ruddy ducks do not seem to like large areas of open water.

Wintering Grounds

The greatest concentrations of ruddy ducks occur in saltwater lagoons, marshes, and bays along the Pacific coast of Mexico. In some winters, the birds may be highly localized. This happened one year near

During courtship, the male ruddy duck cocks his tail upwards and rapidly pumps his head up and down.

Acapulco, Mexico, when 107,000 ruddies were counted offshore. At the time, this may have been more than a third of all the ruddy ducks in North America.

Diet and Feeding Habits
Ruddies, like so many prairie ducks, eat a mixed diet of aquatic plants and insects including diving beetles, dragonfly nymphs, water boatmen, amphipods, and the larvae of midges and caddisflies.

Breeding Biology
The courtship of this attractive duck is amusing to watch. The cocky little drake could easily be mistaken for a windup toy, especially when he performs his "bubbling" sequence, the major display used by courting males. In Volume 3 of *Handbook of North American Birds* the display is described in great detail. "The drake sits high in the water, neck swollen, head held as high as possible, with his tail angled forward so that its tip is near his nape. Then the head is drawn down 6 to 12 times in increasing tempo and, each time, the bill is slapped against the breast producing a hollow tapping sound … the bill striking the feathers near the waterline forces air from among the feathers into the water and bubbles form around

the breast." More than 40 bubbling displays may be performed by a single male in just 20 minutes. The vigor and frequency of the bubbling display apparently reflect the dominance of the male. Conclusion: top drakes really bubble.

Their nest is a floating platform of plant materials anchored to cattails or rushes. Sometimes the ducks will use an old coot nest or an abandoned muskrat house. When water levels are unstable and neighboring nests become flooded, a nest that is still high and dry may be used by multiple females. In one such "dump nest" a researcher found 80 eggs. Typically, a clutch of six to eight eggs is laid in June and is incubated entirely by the female. Once the ducklings hatch, the hen stays with her brood for three to four weeks, then leaves to molt.

Trivia Tidbit
The ruddy duck probably has more regional names than any other prairie duck. Some of the more colorful ones include: "batter-scoot," "noddy," "cock-tail," "hickory-head," "paddy-whack," "quill-tailed coot," "sleepy dick," "rudder bird," "hard-headed broadbill," "dumpling duck," and "bumblebee buzzer." One book listed 70 common names. It's easy to understand why researchers use scientific names to avoid confusion.

Canada Goose

Branta canadensis

Family Details

Waterfowl Family, 147 species worldwide,
20 prairie species

*See Northern Pintail for a general discussion
of the Waterfowl Family.*

Field Identification

The familiar Canada goose has a black head and neck
with a large, white cheek patch. In flight, the characteristic V-formation and the familiar honking makes
this goose the best known of its kind. The subspecies
that nests in the prairies is the "giant Canada," *Branta
canadensis maxima*, the largest of all the 10 or 11
races of Canada geese in North America. An average
male giant Canada weighs 5.5 kilograms (12 lb.), but
some record holders have tipped the scales at twice
that weight.

Where to Find

The goose frequents marshes, sloughs, lakes, and
rivers throughout the prairies.

Wintering Grounds

Most Canadas winter on inland lakes and waterways
in the southern United States.

Diet and Feeding Habits

The Canada goose is a vegetarian that savors the
stems and shoots of sedges, grasses, and many aquatic
plants. They also relish grain crops. And as every
golfer knows, Canada geese love Kentucky bluegrass.
The birds love it so much that they always leave a
special thanks for the greenskeeper to scrape off his
boots. On land, Canadas feed by grazing as they walk
along, and on the water they may upend like dabbling
ducks or just submerge their head and neck to reach
juicy underwater plants.

Breeding Biology

April flights of migrating Canada geese brighten the
hearts of everyone, and herald the return of spring.

*The wingspan
of a prairie
Canada goose
may exceed
1.8 meters
(6 ft.).*

Of the four species of geese that commonly fly over the prairies, only the Canada goose nests here. Nest building often begins in early May, and the finished product is a mound of vegetation hidden among cattails and bulrushes in shallow water or built on a small island for protection. Canadas also like to nest on top of abandoned muskrat and beaver lodges, and sometimes the geese will even use an old raptor's nest, setting up a highrise homestead 15 meters (50 ft.) up in a tree. To avoid coyotes and foxes some Canada geese, along the South Saskatchewan River, nest on inaccessible cliff ledges. The four to seven creamy white eggs hatch after about a month, and the adults immediately move their brood of golden goslings to the water, for safety. The goslings stay with the parents all summer and may even accompany them on their autumn migration. Most Canadas have left the prairies by the end of October.

Snow Goose

Chen caerulescens

A blue-plumaged snow goose may mate with a partner of the same color or one that is all white.

Family Details
Waterfowl Family, 147 species worldwide, 20 prairie species

See Northern Pintail for a general discussion of the Waterfowl Family.

Field Identification
The snow geese that migrate through the prairies occur in two plumage variations. Three-quarters or more of the birds are all white except for large black areas on the tips of their wings. The remaining ones, the so-called "blue geese," have a white head and upper neck and a bluish gray body. White and "blue" varieties of snow geese mix freely, and flocks usually contain both color variations. Snow geese often fly in undulating lines, and for this reason some hunters call them "wavies."

Geese that have fed in coastal tidal areas frequently have the white feathers on their face stained a rusty-orange by the iron minerals in the mud.

Where to Find
In April and early May, large flocks of snow geese fly north over the prairies, returning again in late September and October. The geese may stop temporarily on large lakes to rest and feed during both their spring and autumn migrations. Some impor-

tant staging areas in the prairies include Delta Marsh in Manitoba, the Quill Lakes in Saskatchewan, and Beaverhill Lake in Alberta.

Wintering Grounds
Snows winter mainly along the Gulf Coast, from the Mississippi River southwest to Tampico, Mexico. Large numbers also winter in the Central Valley of California and in Bosque Del Apache Wildlife Refuge in New Mexico.

Diet and Feeding Habits
During migration over the prairies, the geese feed on newly sprouted grasses and waste grain in stubble fields.

Breeding Biology
Snow geese nest along the western coast of Hudson Bay and throughout the High Arctic. They are the most abundant goose in the Arctic, numbering in the millions, and commonly breed in large colonies on the open tundra. The largest colony, containing 460,000 birds, is on the Great Plain of the Koukjduak on southwestern Baffin Island. The geese lay four or five white eggs. These are incubated mainly by the female while the male stands guard nearby. The goslings hatch after 24 days and are flying by the time they are seven weeks old.

Tundra and Trumpeter Swans

Cygnus columbianus and *Cygnus buccinator*

Family Details
Waterfowl Family, 147 species worldwide, 20 prairie species

See Northern Pintail for a general discussion of the Waterfowl Family.

Field Identification
Swans are large, long-necked, all-white birds with black beaks. The birds have no black on their wingtips as do snow geese and white pelicans. Although the trumpeter swan is the larger of the two species, the swans are difficult to distinguish in the field. At close range, a small yellow patch may be visible in front of the eye of most tundra swans.

Trumpeter swans, on the other hand, often have a red line on the upper edge of their lower beak.

Where to Find
The greatest numbers of both species of swans pass through the prairies in April and October. Tundra swans are the more numerous of the two. They nest in the Arctic and fly over the prairies during spring and autumn migrations. During migration, they often stop for a week or two in selected sloughs and lakes, to feed and rest. For example, thousands of tundra swans stop every year at Beaverhill Lake in Alberta.

Trumpeter swans are the largest and rarest swan in the world and are still listed as a vulnerable species in Alberta. No trumpeter swans nest in the prairies, the closest breeding areas being northeastern British Columbia and the sloughs and lakes around Grande Prairie, in west-central Alberta.

Wintering Grounds
Most of the tundra swans that wing their way across prairie skies spend the winter along the Pacific Coast, from Washington to California. In contrast, the primary wintering area for prairie trumpeters is a small area in Montana and Idaho.

During migration, snow geese often travel at night and spend the daylight hours foraging in stubble fields.

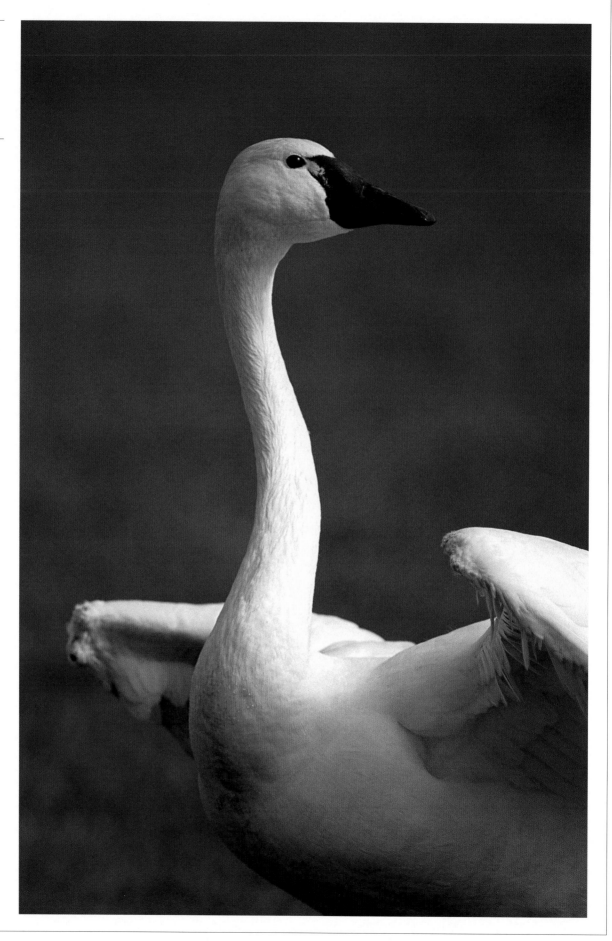

The tundra swan uses the bony corners of its wings to defend itself against predators as well as rival swans.

These trumpeter swans are engaged in a vociferous mutual display—one of the swans' many courtship behaviors.

Diet and Feeding Habits

Both species of swans eat a variety of aquatic plants. Their long necks and strong beaks enable them to reach down and uproot plants that smaller waterfowl, namely ducks and geese, are unable to reach. Swans also use their strong legs and the sharp claws on their large, webbed feet to dig up underwater vegetation. When accompanied by cygnets, parent swans will paddle in place to flush uprooted plants to the surface, where they are easier for the young swans to reach.

Breeding Biology

Both species of swans mate for life, pairing when they are three to four years old. The pairs show a strong attachment to their nesting grounds and return to the same area every year to raise their chicks. Trumpeters may even use the same nest several years in succession, adding new cattails, grasses, and reeds each breeding season until the nest mound becomes as large as a muskrat house. Swans are fiercely aggressive around their nest, and usually there is just one pair on each lake, unless the lake is very large. These short-tempered birds will attack intruders unmercifully. Swans readily chase geese and ducks out of their

territories, and if they catch trespassers, they may trample and bite them repeatedly. In two reported incidents, tundra swans killed six-week-old goslings that accidentally strayed into their territories. The aggressive nature of these large, powerful birds helps them to protect their eggs and offspring from foxes, coyotes, ravens, and gulls.

Swans lay five or six eggs, which the female incubates alone for about a month. The cygnets hatch in June and are on the wing by late summer. The young swans migrate south with their parents in October.

Trivia Tidbit

By the turn of the century, trumpeter swans were nearly extinct, having been hunted relentlessly for food and feathers. By 1930, the only known breeding population was in Yellowstone National Park in Wyoming. There were also a few remnant flocks left in Montana, Alaska, and Alberta. As a result, a joint U.S. and Canadian restoration program was started, and trumpeter numbers slowly began to increase. Today, after nearly 70 years of protection, roughly 600 trumpeters migrate through southern Alberta annually, and continent-wide there are now over 20,000 of these magnificent swans.

The bare skin on a turkey vulture's face keeps gore from soiling the bird's head when it feeds on carrion.

Turkey Vulture

Cathartes aura

Family Details

New World Vulture Family, 7 species in North and South America, 1 prairie species

The vultures are large soaring birds with broad wings. The family includes the Andean condor of South America, one of the largest flying birds in the world. Large male condors can weigh up to 15 kilograms (33 lb.) and have a wingspan over 3 meters (10 ft.). The vultures are nature's cleanup crew, and feed almost entirely by scavenging the bodies of dead animals. They rarely kill prey themselves.

Surprisingly, the New World vultures are not closely related to the vultures of Africa and Asia, even though the two groups are similar in appearance and lifestyle. DNA analysis suggests that storks are the closest relatives of the New World vultures.

Field Identification

The expression "beautiful from afar, but far from beautiful" is how I would describe the turkey vulture.

At close range, the bird's featherless head covered with wrinkled red skin is hard to find attractive. In flight, however, the vulture's true beauty literally soars. Rising aloft on a plume of warm air, the turkey vulture is a graceful, skilled aeronaut. I have watched them float, seemingly effortlessly, for nearly an hour and never flap a wing. The broad V flight profile of this large, dark bird, seen especially when it banks on a turn, is the surest way to distinguish the turkey vulture from any of the soaring hawks of the prairies.

Where to Find

The turkey vulture is an uncommon breeder in the southern prairies of Canada. It can be seen drifting over remote stretches of the Red Deer, Milk, and South Saskatchewan Rivers. Since the 1950s, turkey vulture numbers have risen all across the northern edge of their range in Canada. The increase in sanitary landfills and road-killed animals is thought to be the reason for this.

Wintering Grounds

Turkey vultures are long-distance soaring migrants. Most prairie breeders probably winter from Mexico to northern South America. They often travel great distances without eating, and they are masters of energy conservation. To save energy, they migrate only by day when favorable thermals and air currents can carry them onwards with as little effort as possible. One spring, I watched a northward procession of turkey vultures soar overhead in Costa Rica. In a two-hour period, several thousand vultures drifted past.

Diet and Feeding Habits

The claws of a turkey vulture are blunt and its feet are rather weak and ill-adapted for grasping prey. As well, the bird's beak, though sharp-edged, is not a killing weapon. For all these reasons, the vulture feeds primarily on carrion, although on their wintering grounds they sometimes prey on hatchling sea turtles. As a rule, the bird is a shy, patient diner and never rushes to feed on a carcass. After all, there is no need to hurry, and if the animal on the menu is not quite dead, it is better to wait for its demise and avoid any accidental injury. The best guarantee for a safe meal is the sweet scent of putrefaction. Turkey vultures are among the few birds with a well-developed sense of smell. In fact, the vulture probably locates most carcasses by scent rather than vision. In the 1930s, petroleum engineers in Texas pumped ethyl mercaptan (the smelly substance wafting from carcasses) into natural gas pipelines. By watching the behavior of local turkey vultures the oil workers could quickly locate leaks in the pipeline.

Breeding Biology

I once found a vulture nest in the Cypress Hills of Saskatchewan. The bird had chosen a small cave on a hillside, a common nest location. The vultures also nest on cliff ledges, and in hollow stumps or logs. Occasionally, they may even raise their young in abandoned buildings. In the 1980s, vultures were found nesting in old farm houses near both Biggar and Preeceville, Saskatchewan.

The nest I found in the Cypress Hills held two gray chicks, which is the usual number for a pair to raise. Turkey vultures may mate with the same partner several years in succession, and in fact, they may pair for life. The birds usually arrive on the prairies in early May and leave again some time in August.

Trivia Tidbit

To cool itself, the turkey vulture urinates on its own legs. The evaporation of the watery whitewash lowers the bird's body temperature. In one experiment, an overheated vulture repeated this messy maneuver 40 times in four hours. As distasteful as this behavior seems, bear in mind that every manual on desert survival advises humans to rub urine on their limbs to cool themselves.

Golden Eagle
Aquila chrysaetos

Family Details

Hawk and Eagle Family, 237 species worldwide, 8 prairie species

This family includes the diurnal birds of prey. The members range in size from huge eagles to robin-sized sparrowhawks. The female is usually larger than the male, a reverse from the usual situation in birds. In some cases, the female may be 50 percent heavier than her mate, and have noticeably larger talons and beak.

Hawks and eagles rely on keen eyesight, perhaps four to eight times more acute than that of humans, to locate prey. They use three main methods to hunt: aerial stalking, soaring, and patient perching. All hawks and eagles have sharp talons, and kill their prey by lethal penetration.

When defending prey, the golden eagle ruffles the feathers on its head and neck, signaling its readiness to fight.

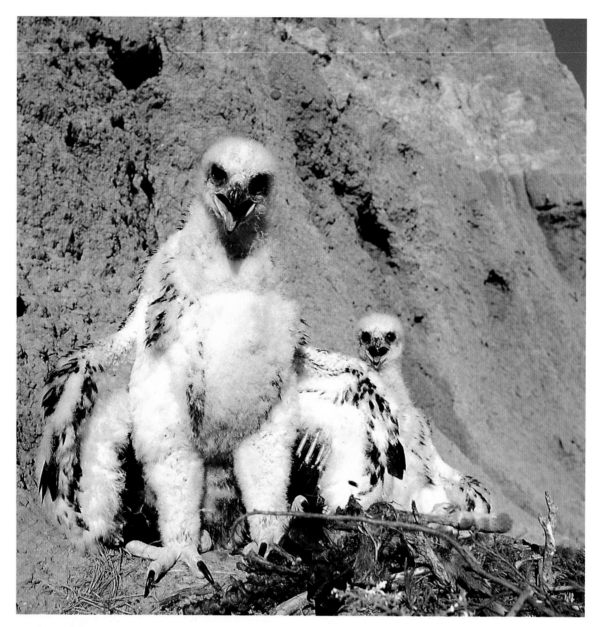

Field Identification

The large size alone—female wingspans can reach
2.3 meters (7.5 ft.)—distinguishes the golden eagle
from every other prairie bird of prey except perhaps a
juvenile bald eagle, which is also big and has dark
feathers. The plumage of the adult golden eagle is
dark brown all over, and the golden feathers on the
nape of its neck are usually visible only at close range.
It takes three to four years for a juvenile eagle to
acquire full adult plumage. While it is maturing, a
juvenile can be identified by a broad white area at the
base of its tail and white patches on the undersides of
its wings.

Where to Find

The majestic golden eagle is an uncommon resident
of native grasslands, badlands, and undisturbed river
valleys throughout the northern prairies.

Wintering Grounds

Some eagles may leave their prairie breeding
grounds, but many stay year-round. Those that leave
probably migrate to grassland and desert areas farther south in the United States, although no
researcher has radio-tracked them to confirm this.

Diet and Feeding Habits

These regal raptors primarily hunt small mammals:
ground squirrels, prairie dogs, jackrabbits, cottontails, and occasionally young deer and pronghorn
fawns. Eagles also hunt grouse, pheasants, and magpies. One nest I examined in southwestern
Saskatchewan contained cormorant remains. Golden
eagles will also eat snakes, especially bullsnakes, and
even venomous prairie rattlesnakes. Carrion is eaten
anytime, but is more important in the birds' winter
diet.

Breeding Biology

Golden eagles may not begin to breed until they are several years old, perhaps as late as age six or seven. Lifelong monogamy is the rule, but as in most animals studied, some pairs divorce after one or more seasons. A breeding pair defends a combined hunting and nesting territory, the size of which depends upon the abundance of prey. In a study in the densely occupied Snake River canyon in Idaho, the eagles had territories of just 57 square kilometers (22 sq. mi.). Eagle territories on the Canadian prairies are likely much larger than this.

Courtship begins as early as late March and early April and includes "sky-dancing," in which one eagle, or both, flies up and down in an undulating course. Most often they nest on cliff ledges and steep badland slopes, and an undisturbed pair may use the same site year after year. Successive generations of golden eagles occupied one nest site for 250 years, from 1689 to 1938, a record! Each year the birds add new sticks to their nest, called an aerie, and it can become massive. The largest I've seen was a meter and a half (5 ft.) in diameter and over 3 meters (10 ft.) high, balanced on a cliff ledge in Yukon. Rarely more than a single chick is raised by a pair. The youngster makes its first flight at around 65 days of age, but continues to be fed for several months after that.

Bald Eagle
Haliaeetus leucocephalus

Family Details

Hawk and Eagle Family, 237 species worldwide, 8 prairie species

See Golden Eagle for a general discussion of the Hawk and Eagle Family.

Field Identification

The adult bald eagle is unmistakable with its dark body and all-white head and tail. Juveniles acquire full adult plumage when they are five or six years old. As they grow, young eagles are a variable patchwork of dark and light feathers, and at this stage they can easily be confused with a golden eagle.

Where to Find

Bald eagles are seen in the prairies mainly during their spring and autumn migrations to and from the northern forests, although sometimes they winter. Ice-free areas in large rivers are attractive wintering sights. Up to 20 eagles, for example, winter annually along the Bow River in Calgary. Farther south in the

The large feathers on a bald eagle's wingtips provide propulsion; the rest of the wing provides lift.

killed mule deer beside the Trans-Canada Highway. Another eagle was dead on the ground nearby. The dead bird probably collided with a vehicle as it tried to fly away. Other winter foods include jackrabbits, cottontails, and waterfowl. One April, I watched an adult bald eagle kill a female mallard that was feeding in a small area of open water in an ice-covered lake. It dragged the struggling duck to shore and ate it alive.

Breeding Biology

Most bald eagles nest along the shorelines of northern lakes in large stick nests at the tops of trees. The eagles return to their breeding grounds as soon as the ice melts, usually in late April and early May, and leave again just prior to freeze-up in October. These familiar raptors mate for life, and a pair returns to the same territory, and often the same nest, year after year. The time from egg laying to fledging of the young takes about four months.

Trivia Tidbit

Both bald and golden eagles can lay up to three eggs, but in most cases, only one or two young survive, depending on the abundance of food brought to the nest. When food is scarce, the largest chick bullies its siblings and gets most of the food. In some cases, the biggest eaglet may even attack and peck its smaller nestmates and kill them. The parent birds never interfere in these family squabbles, and the dead chicks are eaten by the family or are simply trampled into the nest.

Northern Harrier

Circus cyaneus

Family Details

Hawk and Eagle Family, 237 species worldwide, 8 prairie species

See Golden Eagle for a general discussion of the Hawk and Eagle Family.

Field Identification

Harriers are a subgroup of raptors with long, narrow wings and a long tail. Their slow, buoyant flight pattern is a repeating sequence of flap-and-glide, close to the ground. Male northern harriers are pearl-gray above and white below, and the females, as much as twice the weight of their mates, are brown above and tan below with dark streaking. In both sexes, the most noticeable field sign is a bright white rump patch.

The dark feathers, beak, and eyes on this juvenile bald eagle are characteristic of a two-year-old bird.

United States important eagle wintering sites include: Monte Vista Wildlife Refuge in Colorado, Quivira National Wildlife Refuge in Kansas, and Squaw Creek National Wildlife Refuge in Missouri.

Wintering Grounds

Migrants passing through the prairies winter mainly in the southern United States. Birds banded in a northern Saskatchewan study wintered in Arizona and Texas.

Diet and Feeding Habits

Anyone who has ever watched a nature documentary on bald eagles knows that the birds eat fish in the summer. Their winter diet, however, is less well known. Like many birds of prey, the "noble" bald eagle will scavenge dead animals: winter-killed deer, pronghorn, and livestock. Two or three eagles may gather and squabble at a single carcass. One winter, I surprised a juvenile bald eagle feeding on a road-

Where to Find

The northern harrier is widespread throughout the prairies. This handsome raptor was formerly known as the marsh hawk, a reflection of the bird's common breeding habitat, though it also frequents rangeland, croplands, and wet prairies.

Wintering Grounds

Most harriers abandon the prairies in October. They continue to hunt on their southward migration, moving from 15 to 100 kilometers (9–60 mi.) a day. Their wintering range extends from the central United States to southern Mexico.

Diet and Feeding Habits

The facial feathers on the harrier form a disk, giving it a distinctly owl-like appearance. Harriers rely heavily on hearing to capture prey, as do many owls. The sharp-eared raptors mainly hunt small rodents, but will also take songbirds, frogs, snakes, and insects such as grasshoppers. In southern Alberta, I watched an adult white-tailed jackrabbit repeatedly run and jump at a low-flying male harrier that was swooping back and forth overhead. When I went closer to investigate, I found three newborn leverets huddled together on the ground. There was a small patch of fresh blood on the grass nearby. Apparently, the harrier had caught one of the young hares earlier and had returned for another.

Breeding Biology

Harriers nest on the ground, and I have found a number of nests in cattail marshes and also in thickets of rose and snowberry bushes out on the dry prairies. In most cases, the hawks have a different mate every year, and when vole numbers are especially high, they show a strong tendency for bigamy, a single male pairing with two females. On rare occasions, an older male may take up to seven female partners!

A female harrier does all the incubation, while the male feeds her. In doing this, some males may catch more than 40 voles in a single day! Harrier chicks hatch after a month or so. For the first week, the female stays with the young continuously, shading them from the heat of the sun and brooding them when it is cold and wet. During this time, the male provisions the entire family. Usually the food deliveries are passed on the wing, and it's exciting to see. The male flies high and drops the prey to the female, who catches it deftly with her taloned foot while cruising in the air beneath him. At seven days of age, the chicks are about three times as large as when hatched, and from then on, both parents hunt to feed the rapidly growing family. During the month before the chicks fledge, a brood of three may receive 388 meals, totalling 28.5 kilograms (63 lb.) of prey—enough voles and mice to warm any farmer's heart.

Ferruginous Hawk

Buteo regalis

Family Details

Hawk and Eagle Family, 237 species worldwide,
8 prairie species

See Golden Eagle for a general discussion of the Hawk and Eagle Family.

Field Identification

The ferruginous is the largest and heaviest hawk in the prairies, and at a distance it can sometimes be confused with an eagle. The adult has a bright rusty back and rump, white chest and belly, and rusty leggings that form a distinct V against the bird's light underparts.

Where to Find

This shy, open-country bird of prey favors badlands and native grasslands. Grazing, cultivation, and the poisoning of small mammals have caused its widespread decline across the prairies. In Canada, the ferruginous hawk breeds only in the southern portions of Alberta and Saskatchewan.

Wintering Grounds

This beautiful hawk winters in the deserts and grasslands of northern Mexico and the southwestern United States from California to Texas.

Diet and Feeding Habits

The ferruginous hawk is a specialist predator of small- to medium-sized mammals including jackrabbits, cottontails, ground squirrels, prairie dogs, and pocket gophers. The method it uses to capture pocket gophers is particularly interesting. Author Dwight Smith described the technique in *Handbook of North America Birds*, Volume 5. "Pocket gophers push up earthen piles while tunnelling. The hawk flies slowly until it discovers a fresh damp pile. Then it alights and waits for a gopher to push close to the surface; then the hawk rises a few feet in the air and comes down stiff-legged onto the loose earth to [capture] the gopher ..." It's unknown whether the hawk uses auditory clues to catch its prey in the same way an owl listens and pounces on the snow to capture a mouse underneath.

Breeding Biology

The ferruginous hawk is extremely wary. An innocent inspection of its nest site, during the building phase or during egg laying and early incubation, may be enough disturbance to cause the bird to desert. In years of food scarcity, the timid hawks are even more sensitive. For these reasons, a ferruginous nest should *never* be approached during the breeding season.

For many years I have kept records of the nest sites chosen by ferruginous hawks in the badland country of southern Alberta. The two most popular locations are the tops of lone trees, and ground nests on the upper edges of steep clay slopes. The nest platforms (examined in the autumn after the nesting season) were usually made of branches and sticks with an inner cup of dried grass. In rangeland, dried chips of cattle dung were often added to the nest. Ground nests can be a meter (3 ft.) or more in diameter and some were that tall. Only golden eagles construct stick nests as large as those of ferruginous hawks. In the 1800s, ferruginous nests were sometimes made of bison bones and lined with the wool of these shaggy prairie beasts.

Pairs establish breeding territories in early April, and by early May they are incubating. The usual clutch contains two to four eggs, but the number varies from one to eight depending on the abundance of prey. The female broods the chicks for three weeks, and after that she helps the male hunt prey for the young. Within two weeks of fledging, the young hawks begin to hunt for themselves, though their parents continue to feed them for several weeks.

This ferruginous hawk has just caught an unwary ground squirrel after a late spring snowstorm.

Swainson's Hawk

Buteo swainsoni

Family Details

Hawk and Eagle Family, 237 species worldwide, 8 prairie species

See Golden Eagle for a general discussion of the Hawk and Eagle Family.

Field Identification

The Swainson's hawk is one of the most common soaring hawks on the prairies. When in flight, the field signs to look for are a dark-headed bird with a brown upper chest, and white or creamy underwings and belly. Usually, the hawk also has a dark band near the end of its tail.

Where to Find

This bird is an open-country raptor, widespread throughout farming country. The range of the Swainson's hawk overlaps that of the red-tailed hawk and the ferruginous hawk. The three raptors lessen competition among themselves by selecting slightly different prairie habitats. The ferruginous prefers badlands and dry rangelands, the red-tail favors the aspen woodlands of coulees, and the Swainson's is found most often in agricultural lands bordered with bushes and trees.

Wintering Grounds

The Swainson's hawk is the marathon migrant among North American birds of prey. Some individuals may make annual round-trip journeys of 22,000 kilometers (13,700 mi.), commuting between prairie Canada and the pampas of northern Argentina. To conserve energy on these long journeys the hawks masterfully exploit thermal updrafts and favorable winds. Each day as the sun heats the earth, columns of warm air rise to the sky. The hawks spread their broad wings and slip into these rising currents to be carried aloft. Hundreds of hawks may circle together to form a "kettle," with some birds circling clockwise, and others counterclockwise. At the top of the updraft, as high as 6000 meters (19,700 ft.), the air cools and loses its lift, and one by one the hawks break out of the circle and glide off in the direction they wish to travel. From one updraft to another, the birds circle and glide their way thousands of kilometers, across the plains, deserts, and rainforests that separate their breeding and wintering grounds. One

Young Swainson's hawks defend themselves with their sharp-taloned feet rather than their beaks.

40

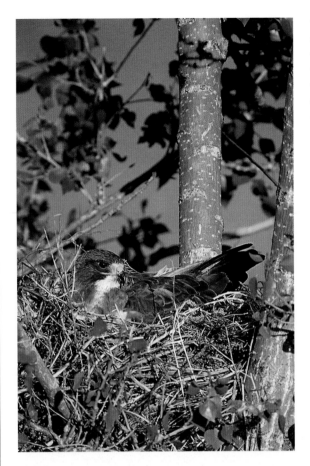

them with their talons. If an intruder sees the dive coming he may roll in midair and lock talons with the attacker. The pair, locked in combat, then spirals to the ground. In most cases, the combatants in these territorial dogfights separate unscathed, but sometimes there are lacerations, broken wings, and even fatal head injuries. The irascible male Swainson's does not limit his aggression to males of his own kind. He may also attack trespassing ferruginous and red-tailed hawks, northern harriers, turkey vultures, golden eagles, great horned owls, crows, and imprudent wildlife photographers.

In a typical year, the monogamous pair raises two young, which fledge in late July.

Red-tailed Hawk

Buteo jamaicensis

Family Details
Hawk and Eagle Family, 237 species worldwide, 8 prairie species

See Golden Eagle for a general discussion of the Hawk and Eagle Family.

Field Identification
The underside of the red-tailed hawk is quite variable in color, and the bird may be puzzling to identify until it flies off, or circles in the distance. The bright rusty upper surface of its tail is unmistakable. The adults give a recognizable two- or three-second scream resembling a steam whistle. Hollywood loves the cry of this hawk and has used it in many films whenever an atmosphere of wilderness is needed, often in settings where no self-respecting red-tail would be found.

Where to Find
The adaptable red-tailed hawk is commonly seen all across North America, in a wide variety of forest habitats. In the prairies, it is found wherever there are groves of tall aspens in which to nest. Usually the red-tail prefers habitats with more trees, and taller trees, than do Swainson's, although both hawks hunt in open country.

Wintering Grounds
The red-tail, like the other common hawks of the prairies, is absent for six months of the year. It winters all across the central and southern United States and northern Mexico.

The female Swainson's hawk does most of the incubation, while her mate feeds her.

female Swainson's from Saskatchewan was tracked by satellites. She left Canada on 22 September and arrived in Argentina 69 days later.

Diet and Feeding Habits
Anytime I have seen a Swainson's with prey in its talons, the unlucky victim was always a Richardson's ground squirrel. On the birds' summer breeding grounds, these tawny little rodents are the number one food, though the hawks also eat pocket gophers, songbirds, and snakes. The Swainson's nests a few weeks later than other prairie hawks, and the timing coincides perfectly with the emergence of young, naive ground squirrels.

Breeding Biology
The Swainson's hawk often builds its flimsy nest of branches and Russian thistle in the top of tall willow bushes on the edge of a field. The shelterbelts surrounding abandoned farmhouses are another popular nest site. Swainson's don't seem to mind living relatively close to humans. In an Alberta study, nearly a quarter of the nests were within 0.5 kilometers (0.3 mi.) of a farmyard.

Adult males establish nesting territories near the same area where they hatched, and they defend these aggressively. They patrol from great heights and will dive on any feathered trespassers, attempting to rake

Diet and Feeding Habits

Most of the time, this hawk hunts from the top of a tree, scanning the surroundings with its sharp eyes. Hares, rabbits, ground squirrels, ducks, songbirds, and bullsnakes are all on the menu. When quarry is spotted, the hawk silently drops from its perch, and flap-and-glides swiftly towards the victim. When the hawk is just 2 to 3 meters (6.5–10 ft) from impact—a mere millisecond—it swings its legs forward and strikes the prey, usually with a single taloned foot. It is not uncommon for larger prey, especially those with sharp teeth, to struggle and bite the hawk. The legs and feet of many red-tails bear the scars of these struggles.

Breeding Biology

The red-tail, like so many large raptors, may use the same nest several years in a row, adding new sticks each season. During nest building, egg laying, and incubation, the pair continues to add fresh aspen branches and other greenery to the nest, sometimes on a daily basis. The purpose of this greenery is unclear, but a number of explanations have been proposed. Fresh green leaves may advertise ownership of a nest and deter trespassers. The leaves may sanitize the nest by covering waste materials, or the foliage may deter parasites by releasing noxious aromatic chemicals.

The family life of the red-tail is similar to that of other prairie hawks. The female does most of the incubation while the male provisions her. The clutch of two or three eggs hatches after about a month, and the chicks are then brooded by the female for another week or so while they become more resistant to the vagaries of the weather. By the time the young hawks are five weeks old, both parents are hunting to feed their voracious appetites. Young red-tails begin to fly when they are six or seven weeks of age, but require another six or seven weeks to learn to hunt and feed themselves.

The color of the widely distributed red-tailed hawk varies from very pale shades to almost black.

Prairie Falcon

Falco mexicanus

Family Details

Falcon and Caracara Family, 61 species worldwide, 5 prairie species

The scavenging caracaras, most of which live in South America, are slow-flying birds of prey that resemble vultures in their lifestyle. The falcons, on the other hand, are fast-flying aerial hunters. Once a falcon locates prey from the air, it descends on its target in a feather-rippling dive, called a stoop. It strikes with a powerful blow of its clenched feet or with a deadly slash of its talons. If the victim is still alive, the falcon ends the ordeal with a lethal bite to the base of the skull using a specialized "tooth," called a tomial tooth, on the edge of its upper beak. The tomial tooth is used like a wedge to force apart the vertebrae, injuring or severing the spinal cord. Raptor researcher Dr. Tom Cade believes that this beak specialization allows the falcons to kill prey larger than they could otherwise tackle.

Field Identification

The prairie falcon is light brown above and whitish underneath with contrasting dark "armpits." The head and back of the prairie is much lighter than that of the peregrine falcon, with which it may be confused. The prairie falcon's flight is usually low, strong, and fast.

Where to Find

The prairie is a denizen of open country, favoring native grasslands, rangelands, and badlands. This remarkable raptor is found throughout the northern prairies.

Wintering Grounds

A few of these attractive falcons remain on the prairies throughout the winter, but many migrate to the plains, deserts, and canyonlands of the western United States.

Diet and Feeding Habits

This versatile predator uses a number of hunting techniques: perch-and-wait, low-level flapping flight to flush prey, or power dives from altitudes of 1000 meters (3300 ft.) or more. Sometimes a crafty falcon will follow a northern harrier from aloft and steal its kill, or capture escaping birds that were flushed by the harrier. In the Canadian prairies, the common prey of this falcon are ground squirrels and songbirds, especially horned larks, mourning doves, meadowlarks, and longspurs.

Breeding Biology

Mates probably associate on the wintering grounds and then return independently in March to the northern prairies, the male arriving a week or two before his partner. In a mild winter, the pair may arrive three to four weeks earlier. The most common nesting site is a cliff ledge, at least 9 meters (30 ft.) up, but not too close to the top, where it could be reached by a nimble-footed coyote or fox. The male prairie falcon, like hawks and eagles, does most of the hunting for his mate, while she incubates the eggs. The two to four white, downy young hatch after a month. The young can fly at six weeks of age, but their parents continue to feed them for at least three weeks after that. Three-quarters of the young die in their first year, most from starvation. The surviving yearlings return the following spring but usually do not breed for at least another year.

The small American kestrel is the only prairie bird of prey that nests in a tree cavity.

American Kestrel

Falco sparverius

Family Details

Falcon and Caracara Family, 61 species worldwide, 5 prairie species

See Prairie Falcon for a general discussion of the Falcon and Caracara Family.

Field Identification

The kestrel, smaller than a blue jay, is the smallest bird of prey in North America. The male and female kestrel differ in coloration, an uncommon trait in birds of prey. The larger female has a rusty back and wings, while her smaller mate has blue-gray wings and a rusty back. Both sexes have a characteristic pair of black streaks on the sides of their face. The birds also have two dark spots on the rear of their neck. It's speculated that these "eye spots" may deter predators from making a rear attack. The kestrel's habit of bob-

bing its head makes these eye spots even more convincing.

Where to Find

The kestrel is numerous and widespread across the prairies. It prefers open terrain, including fields, rangelands, and badlands. It commonly perches on telephone wires and fences.

Wintering Grounds

Some kestrels may winter in the Canadian prairies, but many migrate to the southern United States. Recently there has been an increasing tendency for

urban kestrels to stay in Canda for the winter. An abundance of easy prey, in the form of house sparrows and starlings, enables the little falcons to fuel themselves against the cold.

Diet and Feeding Habits

The kestrel may either still-hunt from an elevated perch, or hover-hunt. Hover-hunting is the most entertaining technique to watch. When prey is sighted, the falcon begins to hover and line up the attack. Usually it is no higher than 25 meters (82 ft.). Sometimes the bird may drop a few meters and continue to hover at a lower height, waiting for its prey to be more vulnerable. Kestrels can hover like this for up to a minute, or longer when the wind speed is high, but the energy costs are great. When the moment is right, the falcon drops like a rock and grasps its prey.

When I started to bird-watch 40 years ago, everyone called the kestrel the "grasshopper hawk" because of its appetite for these insects. On the prairies, this dextrous little falcon commonly catches the large red- and yellow-winged grasshopper species, as well as dragonflies, beetles, butterflies, crickets, and wolf spiders. It also hunts songbirds, voles, mice, and bats.

Breeding Biology

The American kestrel may be the smallest bird of prey, but it has the largest sexual appetite. One pair mated ten times in an hour. Another couple mounted 14 times in just 36 minutes! Researchers estimate that a pair may copulate 690 times, even though twice a week would be often enough to fertilize the eggs. It's likely that frequent copulation reinforces the bond between the pair, a strategy that also seems to apply to our own species.

Kestrels usually nest in cavities. They may choose rock crevices in lofty cliffs, abandoned woodpecker holes, or natural hollows in aspen and cottonwood trees. Both parents incubate the clutch of four to six eggs, but the male's participation varies between individuals. In some cases, the male may incubate for as much as four hours, doing a morning and an afternoon stint. In other instances, he may sit on the nest only at night. The eggs hatch after about 28 days.

Raptor researchers Noel and Helen Snyder observed: "Like the young of many hole-nesting birds, young kestrels are relatively noisy, apparently deriving considerable security against predators from the nature of their nest sites." The young falcons first fly and leave the nest at one month of age, but they may return to the cavity at night with their mother for several weeks afterwards.

Peregrine Falcon

Falco peregrinus

Family Details

Falcon and Caracara Family, 61 species worldwide, 5 prairie species

See Prairie Falcon for a general discussion of the Falcon and Caracara Family.

Field Identification

The adult peregrine is a large falcon, dark gray on top and heavily barred on its undersides. The bird's head and face are dark, and it has distinctive "sideburns"

This female peregrine is brooding her young on a highrise building in the center of Calgary, Alberta, a city of 800,000 people.

Even at three weeks of age, young female peregrines can be distinguished from males by their large feet .

on the sides of its neck. Female peregrines are larger and about 30 percent heavier than males; otherwise the sexes are similar in appearance. Juveniles are brown above and buff underneath with heavy streaking, and also have the dark sideburns.

Where to Find

Historically, peregrines nested on cliffs along most of the large rivers in the northern prairies. After World War II, the indiscriminate use of the pesticide DDT gradually poisoned the birds. They failed to reproduce, and their numbers slowly declined. In 1975, the falcons were officially declared "extirpated" south of the boreal forest and east of the Rocky Mountains. Since then, the use of DDT has declined worldwide and captive-bred peregrines have been successfully reintroduced into the Canadian prairies, with many pairs choosing to breed in the urban core of cities such as Calgary, Edmonton, Saskatoon, Regina, and Winnipeg. The urban settings were sometimes chosen for release sites to lessen the danger from great horned owls, which often prey on young peregrines.

In 1995, wild peregrines finally nested again in the native Canadian prairies along the Red Deer and Bow Rivers in Alberta, after an absence of nearly 30 years. In recent years, the adaptable peregrine has also repopulated the western regions of Montana, Wyoming, and Idaho, as well as the Colorado Plateau.

Wintering Grounds

The exact wintering range of the prairie peregrine is not well known, but it is likely that most of the birds migrate to Mexico, Central America, and South America. Nestlings banded in Alberta have been recovered as far south as Belize and Columbia. The nesting falcon whose photo appears on page 45 was photographed on the 15th-floor ledge of a high-rise building in the center of Calgary in June 1998. Dr. Gordon Court, a wildlife biologist with Alberta Environmental Protection, told me the remarkable story about this bird. Two years earlier, researchers noticed mysterious black electrical tape wrapped around the band on the bird's left leg, and they captured it to investigate. Under the tape, a condom wrapper contained a slip of paper with the name and address of a German shipping company. The biologists were intrigued and wrote to the company in Bremen, Germany, to unravel the story. Apparently, one of the company's ships had been 160 kilometers (100 mi.) offshore from Tampico, Mexico, during a November hurricane, and the falcon had taken refuge on the ship. A Filipino seaman who loved birds had captured the falcon and taken it to his cabin to shelter the bird from the storm. Before releasing it he had attached the message to its leg.

Diet and Feeding Habits

The fast-flying peregrine is a versatile aerial hunter, and at one time or another has probably preyed on every small- and medium-sized bird on the prairies. Urban peregrines commonly hunt pigeons, starlings, robins, and house sparrows—birds that do well in heavily populated human environments. The big-city peregrines surprised Dr. Court with some unexpected quarry: American coots, eared grebes, red crossbills, sora rails, blue-winged teals, and even escaped budgies and cockatiels. Dr. Court thinks a foraging falcon may hunt as far as 40 kilometers (25 mi.) from its nest, reaching the agricultural lands and wetlands that surround most cities.

The peregrine is so beloved by falconers because of one of its hunting strategies—the feather-rippling power dive, called a stoop. An attacking falcon tucks its tapered wings, and falls like a thunderbolt from the floor of the sky. In such a dive, the peregrine is the fastest bird on wings, reaching potential speeds in excess of 300 kilometers per hour (180 mph). The victim is killed with a smashing blow from the peregrine's semi-clenched feet or is slashed to death with its trailing rear talons.

Breeding Biology

Most peregrines are back on the prairies aggressively defending their nesting territories by the middle of April. The birds can be extremely faithful to their nest site, returning year after year. One female has been using the same location on a building in downtown Edmonton, Alberta, for 12 years in a row.

Typically, a peregrine nest is nothing more than a scrape on the ledge of a cliff or a high-rise building. The birds usually lay three or four rusty, speckled eggs. The female does most of the incubating, and for the 33 days it takes for the eggs to hatch, the male does much of the hunting, and feeds his mate. Young peregrines begin to fly at around 40 days of age, but their parents feed them for at least a month afterwards.

Ruffed Grouse
Bonasa umbellus

Family Details
Grouse Family, 17 species worldwide,
4 prairie species

The grouse are a group of large, chickenlike birds that spend most of their time on the ground. They are reluctant fliers. All have relatively small wings

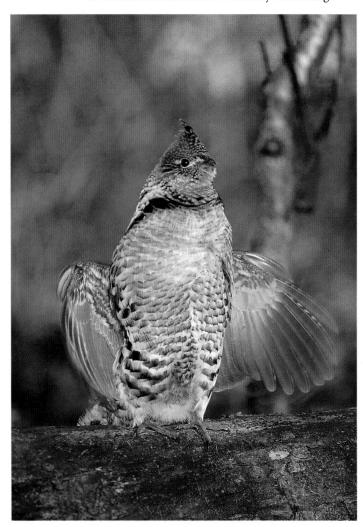

A male ruffed grouse may drum from three or four different sites in his territory.

for their body size, so their takeoffs are noisy, and flushed birds explode into flight with a roar of wings. Once on the wing, they fly close to the ground with bursts of rapid wingbeats, and they usually land after only a short time in the air.

The Grouse Family evolved in the cold climates of the Northern Hemisphere, and they are superbly adapted to endure the worst winter weather. Grouse have thick, dense plumage, comprising as much as 20 percent of their body weight. They have protective feathers over their nostrils and on their legs and toes.

In winter, they grow a fringe of scales along the edge of their toes; this increases the surface area of their feet and functions like a snowshoe.

Field Identification
The plumage of all the prairie grouse is a mottled mixture of earth tones, and one of the easiest ways to separate the species is by the appearance of the bird's tail. The ruffed grouse has a finely striped tail with a broad, black band near the tip. The black neck "ruff" of the grouse, from which the bird derives its name, is present in both sexes, but it is usually hidden and is most visible in males during spring courtship.

Where to Find
The ruffed grouse is widespread throughout Canada. The bird's range corresponds almost exactly with that of two species of deciduous trees: the quaking aspen and balsam poplar. In the prairies, the grouse is a frequent inhabitant of coulees and streamside woodlands.

Wintering Grounds
The ruffed grouse is a year-round resident of the prairies, and most spend the entire year within a relatively small home range, usually less than 10 hectares (25 acres). Adult males are particularly sedentary. They may spend their entire lives within a 200-meter (650-ft.) radius of their main drumming log.

Diet and Feeding Habits
The most important winter foods of the ruffed grouse are aspen buds and catkins, which is no surprise, given the birds' close association with these trees. During the rest of the year, the grouse eat the buds, flowers, leaves, and berries of more than 500 kinds of plants. Young grouse chicks need great amounts of fat and protein to fuel their growth and eat large numbers of insects and spiders as a result.

Breeding Biology
The drumming of the male ruffed grouse in early April is familiar to everyone who walks through a coulee after the cold, quiet days of winter. The drumming is produced by the rapid beating of the bird's wings against the air. A typical drumming session lasts seven to ten seconds and is repeated, on average, every four minutes. Popular drumming sites are tree roots and fallen tree trunks, and the same site may be used year after year for as long as the grouse lives. A human can hear a "drummer" half a kilometer (0.3 mi.) away, and I always thought it must be easy for a great horned owl, one of the grouse's main predators, to listen and locate the birds. It turns out, however, that the frequency of the grouse's drumming is below the hearing range of the owl.

After a female is lured to a drumming log and she mates with the owner, the male ruffed grouse has nothing more to do with her. The female lays 9 to 12 creamy eggs in a shallow scrape under shrubbery or in some bushes, and incubates them without any help for 23 days. An incubating hen spends more than 90 percent of her time on the nest, leaving only two or three times in a day to feed. In late May, the chicks hatch, and within a day the female leads them away from the nest. The young grouse feed themselves from the moment of hatching, and they stay with their mother until the family breaks up in early autumn.

Sharp-tailed Grouse

Tympanuchus phasianellus

Family Details
Grouse Family, 17 species worldwide,
4 prairie species
See Ruffed Grouse for a general discussion of the Grouse Family.

Throughout April, male sharp-tails gather at traditional dancing grounds, called leks, to strut and coo.

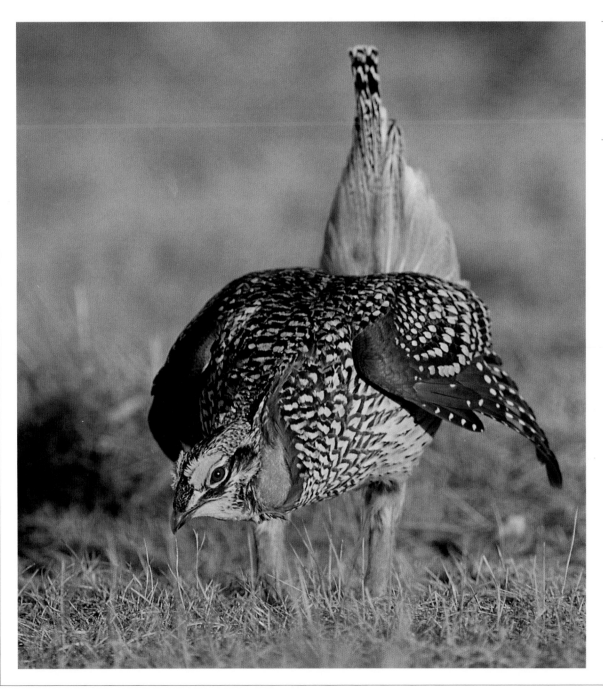

Field Identification

The sharp-tail's name is a clue to the easiest way to identify this cryptically colored prairie bird. The grouse has a pointed tail with white patches on the edges, visible when the bird flushes. The male and female are similar in appearance, except during courtship when the males pump themselves up and display engorged yellow eye combs and vibrant purple throat sacs.

Where to Find

The sharp-tail is found throughout the northern prairies. It favors open grasslands mixed with shrubbery such as prairie rose, snowberry, and wolf willow.

Wintering Grounds

The sharp-tailed grouse is a year-round prairie resident. In winter, the birds form flocks of up to 100 birds.

Diet and Feeding Habits

About 90 percent of the grouse's diet consists of the fruits, seeds, flowers, and buds of plants. Less common foods include beetles, grasshoppers, and crickets. Insects are most important to young chicks, and compose the bulk of their diet for the first four to six weeks of life.

Breeding Biology

Grouse are one of my favorite groups of birds, and every spring I try to witness the courtship of at least one of the family. Many years ago, I wrote these words in *Married to the Wind: A Study of the Prairie Grasslands*: "In the Great Sand Hills of southwestern Saskatchewan March is an empty time. The landscape is leached of colour, and the bite of winter lingers as deer and pronghorn move slowly, rationing their strength. Silence pervades, the insects are locked in hibernation, and the songbirds are still a month away. The ground is frozen and brittle underfoot, the plants firmly held in check. But on a grassy knoll, life refuses to be restrained, and the sharp-tails dance. Each spring, sharp-tailed grouse assemble on ancestral dancing grounds to re-enact their courtship ritual. The males coo, cluck, and strut. With their heads down and their tails pointed to the sky, they rapidly stomp their feet, and little clouds of dust erupt around them. The birds vibrate across the ground like wound-up toys; they run feverishly for a moment, and then suddenly stop." Thirty or 40 males may gather on a dancing ground half the size of a football field. Each male defends his own small patch of prairie. One by one, female grouse wander through the cluster of males, assessing the dancers for qualities only they can detect, looking for a mate. Once the hen makes her choice she mates just once and then leaves.

Sharp-tails nest on the ground, and every nest I have found was hidden in a clump of rose bushes or snowberry. The hen lays 10 to 13 plain, buff-colored eggs. As in all grouse, the eggs hatch within hours of each other and the precocious chicks are led away from the nest by the female. The down-covered young are a mottled patchwork of gold, brown, and black, and blend perfectly with the dried grasses of the prairie. The young become independent by two months of age.

Trivia Tidbit

A clutch of grouse, pheasant, or waterfowl eggs usually hatches within hours of each other. I discovered how they do this in the 1995 edition of Frank Gill's fascinating textbook *Ornithology*. Remarkably, the chicks of these birds synchronize their hatching by clicking to each other while they are still inside the shell. In mallard ducks, for example, older chicks that are about to hatch click at a rate between 2 and 60 times per second. This relatively slow rate stimulates the younger chicks in the clutch to get cracking, and accelerate their hatching effort. Younger chicks, on the other hand, click at higher rates, usually over 100 times per second. This, in turn, slows down the struggles of the older chicks, who as a result may delay breaking free for more than 33 hours. The mechanisms of the natural world are sometimes truly extraordinary.

Sage Grouse
Centrocercus urophasianus

Family Details

Grouse Family, 17 species worldwide,
4 prairie species

See Ruffed Grouse for a general discussion of the Grouse Family.

Field Identification

The sage grouse is the largest grouse in North America. A large male can weigh over 3 kilograms (6.5 lb.), five times as much as a ruffed grouse. The bird's size alone is usually enough to identify it, as well as its long tail feathers and black belly.

Where to Find

The sage grouse lives in the driest areas of the northern prairies wherever sagebrush grows. In the American plains, the greatest numbers occur in Wyoming, Idaho, and Montana. In Canada, the grouse is limited to the extreme southwestern corner of Saskatchewan and the southeastern corner of Alberta, an area referred to as Palliser's Triangle. Sadly, the sage grouse is in big trouble in Canada, and is designated as an endangered species. Biologists estimate that fewer than 500 breeding pairs remain.

Wintering Grounds
The sage grouse is a year-round resident of the prairies. In winter, it concentrates wherever exposed sagebrush is found.

Diet and Feeding Habits
The sweet scent of sagebrush on a summer morning is one of the great pleasures of a walk on the short-grass prairies. This aromatic plant is nutritious, retains its leaves throughout the winter, and is tall enough to reach above the snow. For these reasons, the leaves of sagebrush constitute nearly 100 percent of the winter diet of the sage grouse. At other times of the year, the grouse eats the leaves of grasses and wildflowers, as well as small numbers of ants, grasshoppers, and beetles. The grinding gizzard of the sage grouse is less muscular than it is in the ruffed and sharp-tailed grouse, and as a result, the sage grouse eats fewer seeds and grains than both of these birds.

Breeding Biology
From March to May, male sage grouse cluster, as do sharp-tails, on traditional dancing grounds, called leks, to display and court females. Each male defends a small territory, sometimes less than 15 meters (50 ft.) across. The handsome suitor spreads his tail, struts, and inflates a large, pendulous throat pouch. In the last moments of the display, the air trapped inside the pouch is suddenly released, producing two

large pops—the grouse version of a satisfied burp. The central territories of a dancing ground are occupied by the oldest, most dominant males, and for a sex-crazed male, the center of the lek is definitely the place to be. Ninety percent of the hens will mate with the few males displaying in the center of the lek. In fact, in a given year, nine out of ten males never lay a feather on a female. They strut and pop in vain, and like many incurable sports fans, they dream of next season.

Female sage grouse, like all prairie grouse, are single mothers. After the male contributes his three seconds of involvement, the hen is on her own. Typically, sage grouse lay seven or eight eggs in a shallow nest at the base of a cluster of sagebrush. Any ground nest is highly vulnerable to mammalian predators, and up to 60 percent of sage grouse eggs are eaten by badgers, coyotes, and ground squirrels. The hen incubates the eggs for 26 days, and afterwards stays with the chicks until they disperse later in the summer.

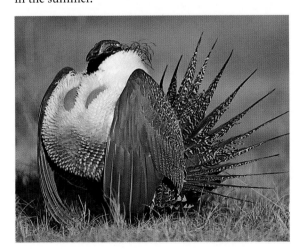

During boundary squabbles, rival male sage grouse may peck their adversaries and beat each other with their wings.

As many as 80 male sage grouse may display together on a dancing ground during spring courtship.

Ring-necked Pheasant

Phasianus colchicus

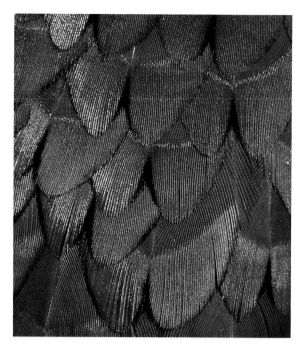

Family Details

Partridge and Pheasant Family,
155 species worldwide, 2 prairie species

Members of this large family are another group of chickenlike birds. They all have strong feet and legs and prefer to walk and run rather than fly. They differ from grouse in having featherless legs and feet, and no feathers around their nostrils. Also, none of these birds has colorful inflatable air sacs, although many species have vibrant wattles and combs. One of the unique features of this family is the presence of sharp spurs on the legs of many of the males. One peacock-pheasant from Malaysia has as many as seven spurs on each leg! Spurs probably function primarily as weapons during fights between rival males, although this explanation is still controversial.

Most species in this family live in Asia or Africa, occupying a wide range of habitats from tropical rainforests to alpine grasslands. They tend to be fairly sedentary and use the same habitat throughout the year. Many of these hardy, adaptable birds have been introduced throughout the world as gamebirds.

The rusty breast feathers of the male pheasant (right) are part of its year-round plumage.
The color of its wattles (below) intensifies when it meets a female or a rival male.

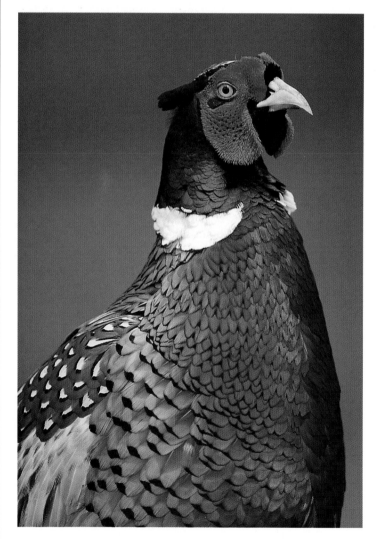

Field Identification

The gaudy male pheasant has a crimson face, metallic green head and neck, white collar, chestnut breast, and a long, tapered tail. The female is a mottled mixture of brown, black, and tan. The hen is best identified by her long tail.

Where to Find

No pheasant or partridge is native to North or South America, and both prairie species, the ring-necked pheasant and the gray partridge, were introduced by hunters in the 1800s. The ring-necked pheasant has prospered in its new home, and the bird is found throughout central North America. In the prairies, the pheasant favors croplands, weedy ditches, shelterbelts, and the shrubby areas along fence lines.

Wintering Grounds

On a sunny day, the sight of a flamboyantly feathered male pheasant running across the snow is enough color to overdose any photographer, and for 20 years I've been chasing that winter image. The pheasant stays on the prairie all winter. In late fall, neighboring birds usually band together, forming flocks of up to 50 individuals. The flocks disband and scatter at the start of the spring breeding season.

Diet and Feeding Habits

The ringed-necked pheasant is a scratch-and-peck feeder. It begins to forage within an hour of sunrise and can be seen moving about anytime during the day. Pheasants are especially fond of waste grain, which explains why they are seen so often in stubble fields. When grain is scarce, the birds eat weed seeds, berries, fresh green shoots, beetles, grasshoppers, crickets, and caterpillars.

Breeding Biology

The male pheasant begins to crow and flutter in early April, hoping to catch the ear of prospective mates. As many as 15 females may be lured to a "crowing area" and mate with the outspoken owner, although the average is only three or four. The male pheasant is extremely territorial, and will chase and fight any rival male that dares to trespass. Although these battles are a wonderful blur of color to witness, they are a serious affair for the participants. Combatants tear at each other's wattles with their sharp-edged beaks and rake each other with their claws and spurs. Occasionally, one of the feathered warriors is killed.

Most hens lay their eggs within the crowing area of their mate. The nest is a shallow hollow on the ground, often hidden in the shrubbery or tall grasses of a roadside ditch. The female alone incubates the 7 to 15 eggs—the largest clutch of any prairie bird. The precocious chicks hatch after 25 to 27 days, and although they can feed themselves, the female still leads them to food, watches for danger, and broods them when they get cold. The young can fly when they are two weeks old.

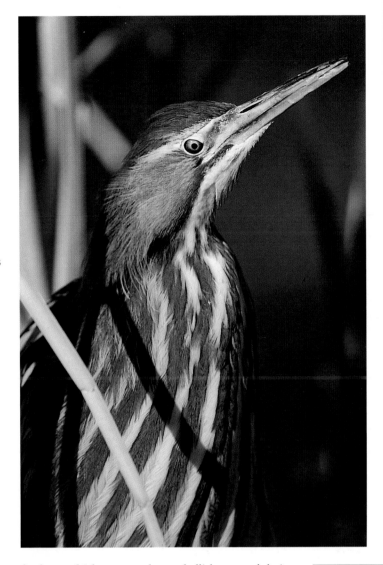

American Bittern

Botaurus lentiginosus

Family Details

Heron Family, 60 species worldwide, 3 prairie species

The family includes the herons, egrets, and bitterns, a familiar group of medium-sized to large wading birds. All of them have long legs, a long, flexible neck, and a long, pointed bill, which they use to grab juicy frogs, fish, crustaceans, and aquatic insects.

During the breeding season, in many species, both the male and female have long, delicate plumes adorning their head, neck, and body. A century ago, hundreds of thousands of herons and egrets were shamelessly slaughtered in North America for their feathers, which were used to embellish women's hair and trim their dresses and hats. In the 1880s, in the heyday of this fashion trend, egret feathers were worth five times their weight in gold! Many herons and egrets nest in large colonies, making their slaughter that much easier. Today, heron and egret numbers have recovered, and the birds are a common sight in the wetlands of the continent.

Field Identification

The American bittern is a chunky, medium-sized wading bird. The sexes are identical, and are mottled brown on their heads and backs with brown and white vertical streaks on their undersides. A black "moustache" line extends down the sides of their neck. When the shy bittern is alarmed, it faces towards the danger, points its beak skyward, and freezes. The vertical streaking on the bird's neck and chest blends in well with the cattails and bulrushes where it lives, and camouflages the bird. The trickster even sways slowly from side to side to imitate the movement of wind-blown reeds.

The low-frequency booming call of the male American bittern may be heard a kilometer (0.6 mi.) away.

Where to Find

The bittern is widespread throughout the prairies, although it is secretive and hard to find. It prefers medium to large marshes with thick stands of tall cattails and bulrushes. The bird rarely leaves the protective cover of vegetation.

Wintering Grounds

The bittern needs year-round access to open water, and those from the prairies may winter from the southern edge of the United States through Mexico and Central America. Most bitterns migrate from the prairies in September or October and return again in early May.

Diet and Feeding Habits

The bittern is most active in the half-light of dusk and dawn. The bird is a master of patience, waiting motionless for long periods to catch its prey. It hunts aquatic beetles and other insects, frogs, toads, salamanders, garter snakes, and even small mammals such as meadow voles. Biologists believe that the vertical streaking on the underside of the bird, though effective camouflage against predators, primarily hides the bird from its prey and helps it to hunt.

Breeding Biology

The eerie call of the male bittern is one of my favorite marsh sounds. Authors James Hancock and James Kushlan described the call in *The Herons Handbook*: "On the breeding ground the American bittern gives a loud booming or pumping sound. The boom of this species is invariably described as resembling the noise of an old-fashioned hand pump, or of hammering a stake into muddy ground, leading to two of the bird's nicknames— 'stake-driver' and 'thunder pumper.'"

The reclusive nature of the bittern makes the bird difficult to observe and study, and many aspects of its biology are still unknown. It seems that males "boom" for at least two reasons: to attract females, and to deter rivals. It's unclear, however, whether a male mates with more than one partner. In one study, researchers found three females nesting in the territory of a single male. The territorial owner may have mated with all of the females, or two of them may have simply moved into the male's territory because his conspicuous booming could distract predators. Even if male bitterns are monogamous, they are still the avian version of the deadbeat dad. The female, alone, builds the family nest of reeds, rushes, and cattails, incubates the three to five eggs, and feeds and broods the young. Young bitterns leave their nest, which is on the ground and hidden in thick cattails, when they are one or two weeks old. After that, the female continues to feed them intermittently for another couple of weeks while the youngsters perfect their hunting skills.

The sunbathing behavior of the great blue heron may reduce skin and feather parasites.

Great Blue Heron

Ardea herodias

Family Details

Heron Family, 60 species worldwide, 3 prairie species

See American Bittern for a general discussion of the Heron Family.

Field Identification

The great blue is the largest heron in North America, and stands about 60 centimeters (24 in.) tall. The bird might better be called the great gray heron since most of its neck and body are medium gray. The heron also has a distinctive black stripe over its eyes. In flight, the great blue holds its neck retracted in an S-shape. The position of its neck is the best way to distinguish the heron from the sandhill crane, another large gray bird with which the heron is sometimes confused. The crane flies with its neck fully extended.

Where to Find

The great blue heron is widespread throughout the prairies and is commonly found along the banks of

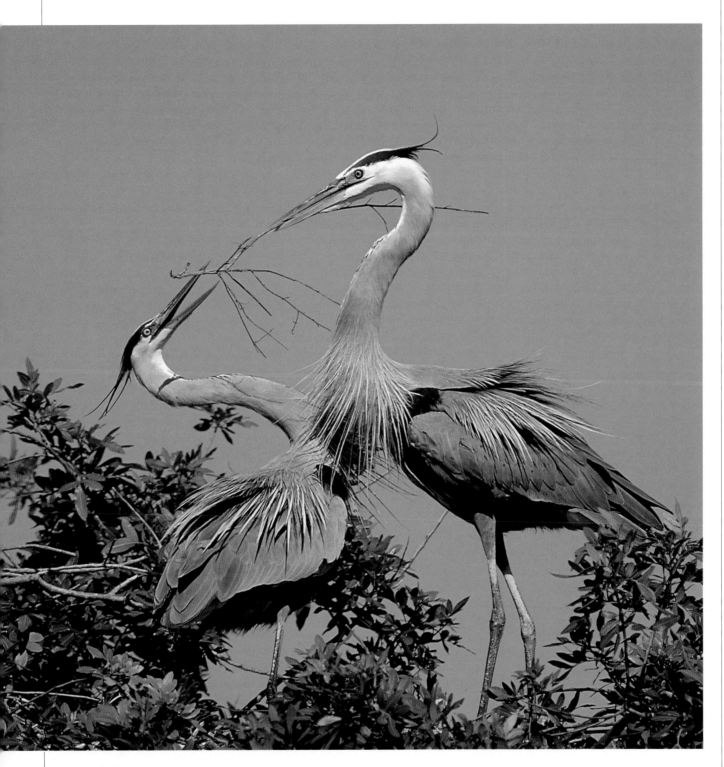

During courtship, the male great blue heron brings branches to his mate who positions them on the nest.

many rivers and streams and around the shorelines of lakes, large sloughs, and irrigation ponds.

Wintering Grounds

Herons from the northern prairies have never been radio-tracked, but it is likely that most of them winter on freshwater wetlands or coastal marshes and shorelines across the southern United States. The birds migrate south in September and October, and many return by the end of March.

Diet and Feeding Habits

The great blue eats mainly fish. It hunts either by walking slowly through the shallows, or by standing still in water up to its belly, waiting for a fish to swim by. The heron, like most wading birds, is not a fussy feeder, and although it may have dietary preferences it will rarely pass up an easy meal. As a result, the great blue also eats aquatic insects, snails, frogs, salamanders, snakes, and any unwary mammal small enough for the bird to swallow whole, including an adult Richardson's ground squirrel. Herons have even been known to tackle muskrats. In one account, a heron battled with one of these chisel-toothed rodents for over an hour before the bird finally killed the muskrat and swallowed it in a single gulp.

Breeding Biology

The great blue heron, which may live for 20 years, pairs with a new partner every spring. When the herons return to the prairies in late March, they may form temporary flocks on "gathering grounds," where they likely choose a mate for the coming season. Courtship includes a number of elaborate displays: sky-pointing, bill-duelling, ceremonial preening, twig-shaking, and bill-clacking.

In the prairies, the great blue nests in small colonies of a dozen pairs or fewer. It usually builds a large nest of sticks, but often a pair may reuse an old nest from a previous season, adding new sticks to the pile. These refurbished nests can become quite bulky and may measure a meter (3 ft.) in diameter, a meter deep, and weigh up to 50 kilograms (110 lb.). Trees and islands are the most popular nesting sites in the prairies, since both offer the herons protection from predatory coyotes and red foxes.

The eggs of the great blue heron are a beautiful greenish blue, and a clutch of four eggs is the most common. Both parents share the four-week incubation, with the female usually taking the night shift. The eggs hatch roughly one to two days apart, so the growing chicks vary greatly in size. When food is scarce the smallest chick starves to death. The antics of wobbly-necked young herons are comical to watch, and their appearance is just as amusing. The bug-eyed young chicks are covered with patchy clumps of gray down that are especially bushy on the top of the bird's head, giving it a punk appearance, as if it had just stuck its toes into a wall socket.

Both parents feed regurgitated globs of food to the chicks, and a pair may make dozens of feeding visits to the nest in a day. The gangly chicks are nearly two months old when they finally begin to fly, and they return to the nest to be fed for another three weeks after that.

Black-crowned Night-heron

Nycticorax nycticorax

Family Details

Heron Family, 60 species worldwide, 3 prairie species

See American Bittern for a general discussion of the Heron Family.

Field Identification

The night-heron is a medium-sized stocky heron, similar in size and build to the American bittern. Both have relatively short legs and a short neck, compared with the tall, stately great blue heron. Male and female night-herons are similar in appearance and have a black cap, black back, gray wings, and creamy underparts. At close range, the birds have attractive ruby-red eyes, which make them unmistakable.

Where to Find

The black-crowned night-heron is the most widespread heron in the world, and is found on every continent except Australia and Antarctica. In the prairies, this adaptable heron is locally common in large sloughs and marshes, but because of its nocturnal habits it is often overlooked. During the peak chick-feeding period the bird may be active during the day, but generally it spends the daylight hours hidden in thick cattails.

Wintering Grounds

Most night-herons leave the prairies by late September. Birds banded in Saskatchewan and Alberta have been recovered in freshwater marshes and mangrove swamps in Mexico, Texas, Florida, and Cuba.

Diet and Feeding Habits

Typically, the night-heron feeds from early evening to early morning. The bird's nocturnal habits reduce competition with the great blue heron and the bittern, which hunt more often in the daylight. The diet of the night-heron has been studied extensively, and as you might predict for a bird with such a cosmopolitan range, it is an opportunistic omnivore. In an Alberta study, the herons ate stickleback fish, leopard frogs, chorus frogs, toads, dragonflies, diving beetles, blackbird nestlings, grasshoppers, crickets, water striders, and meadow voles. The night-heron hunts by slowly stalking the shallows, or by standing motionless, waiting patiently for prey to move within range of its lightning jab.

Breeding Biology

The black-crown is faithfully monogamous during the breeding season, but mates with a different partner every year. The birds nest colonially, building platforms of twigs and weed stalks in the middle of dense stands of cattails and bulrushes. In the prairies, night-herons often nest close to noisy colonies of Franklin's gulls. The aggressive gulls may provide the herons with protection by mobbing egg predators such as crows, magpies, and ring-billed and California gulls. The black-crown repays the Franklin's gulls by eating their unattended chicks. No one ever said nature was fair.

In Alberta, egg laying begins in late April and early May, earlier than for other prairie herons. The birds lay three or four greenish blue eggs, and the parents share the 23- to 26-day incubation period. Both adults also feed the young. The insatiable chicks grab the parent's beak to stimulate it to regurgitate warm, gooey meals. As the chicks get larger, the parents simply dump food on the nest and the young gobble it up. Veteran heron researcher Dr. Bill Davis Jr. wrote: "Young chicks are quite aggressive, and often deposit their most recent meal on an investigator"—a polite way of saying they puke and peck. Night-heron nestlings fledge by the time they are six or seven weeks old, but they continue to beg for food from their parents and any other adult they encounter. At this age, most of the time they are unsuccessful.

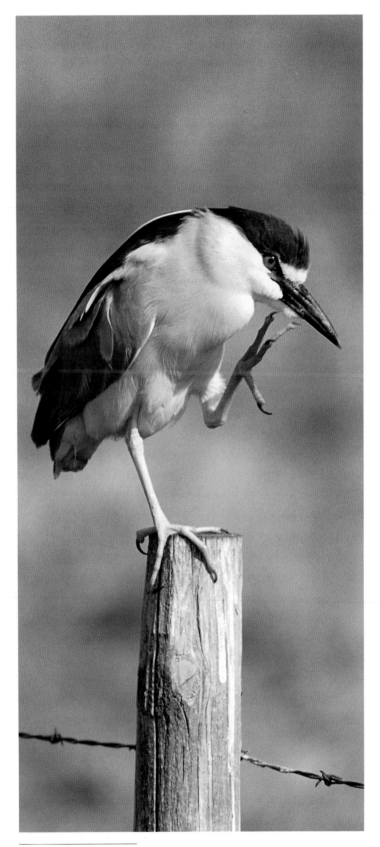

The large eyes on the black-crowned night-heron are an adaptation for nocturnal foraging.

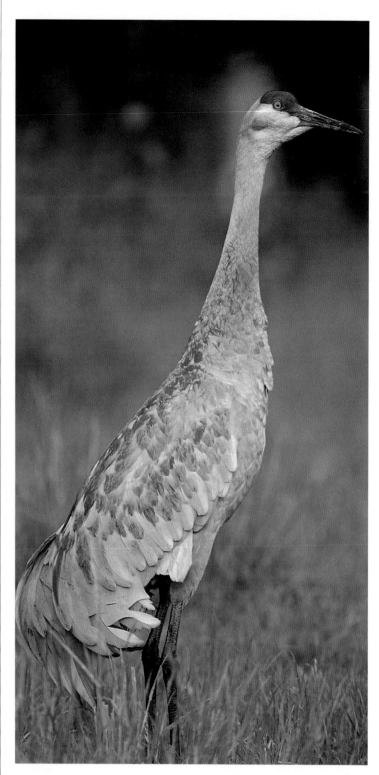

Sandhill Crane

Grus canadensis

Family Details

Crane Family, 15 species worldwide, 2 prairie species

Cranes are large birds, all of whom are adapted for life around water, and have long legs and necks. The family includes the tallest of all flying birds, the sarus crane of India and Australia, which is slightly taller than 1.5 meters (5 ft.), and slightly taller than my wife on a good hair day.

Cranes bugle and trumpet, producing some of the most delightful wild music in the natural world. The windpipe, in most of these birds, is exceptionally long and coils inside the breastbone. The long wind-pipe amplifies their calls, and many species can be heard several kilometers away.

Cranes are long-lived birds; some may live to 30 years of age. Generally, these birds mate for life. Their longevity, faithfulness, elegant stature, and elaborate courtship dances have elevated these majestic birds to symbols of good fortune in Asia. Nonetheless, four Asian species are currently vulnerable or endangered. Closer to home, the situation is no better. The North American whooping crane narrowly escaped extinction in the 1940s. Today, despite more than 50 years of intense protection and management, the wild population of whooping cranes is still endangered, and numbers fewer than 200 birds. The deterioration and loss of wetlands is the biggest threat facing cranes in the next millennium.

Field Identification

The sandhill crane is a tall, gray bird with a feather-less crimson crown, and white cheeks. Juvenile birds are reddish brown, but acquire adult plumage by the time they are one year old. Cranes fly with their long necks fully extended. Another large gray bird, the great blue heron, which may be mistaken for a sand-hill, flies with its neck folded in an S-shape and its head nestled between its shoulders.

Where to Find

The sandhill formerly nested in the prairies. It now stops only to roost and feed in the area, as it passes through on its annual spring and autumn migrations in April and September. Commonly, the birds roost in shallow, open wetlands and feed in nearby stubble fields. In the autumn, large numbers of sandhills regularly stop at Last Mountain Lake, the Quill Lakes, and the Kindersley area of southern Saskatchewan, as well as the Jasper-Pulaski Game Management Area in Indiana.

When alerted, the wary sandhill crane stretches to its full height of 1.4 meters (4.5 ft.).

Wintering Grounds

Virtually all of the cranes migrating through the prairies winter in New Mexico and Texas. The birds migrate during the day, taking off a few hours after sunrise and landing one or two hours before sunset. Travelling in V-formation, and at speeds up to 80 kilometers per hour (50 mph) with a tailwind, they cover about 250 kilometers (155 mi.) a day. Young sandhills travel with their parents on their first migration. In cranes, unlike most birds, knowledge of migration routes and wintering sites is not instinctual.

Diet and Feeding Habits

The crane is a big bird with a correspondingly big appetite, which it satisfies by eating a great variety of foods. Its diet includes berries, waste grain, insects, birds' eggs, nestlings, frogs, snakes, and small mammals.

Breeding Biology

Adult sandhills usually do not breed until they are two or three years old, and some first-timers may be seven before they finally nest. Courtship begins on the wintering grounds, and includes an elaborate "dance," in which partners repeatedly leap into the air with their wings outstretched, bugling in excitement.

Most of the cranes passing through the prairies are bound for muskeg bogs in the boreal forest or the soggy Arctic tundra. Sandhill eggs are olive-colored, splattered with dark brown and rusty blotches. The usual clutch of two is laid on a large mound of vegetation, a meter (3 ft.) or more across, and 15 to 20 centimeters (6–8 in.) high. Both adults share in the month-long incubation of the eggs. Typically, egg number one hatches two to three days ahead of egg number two. By the time the second chick arrives, the older chick is much larger than the new arrival, and a battle for survival begins. The two chicks often fight and peck each other until one of them, usually the older one, drives away its younger sibling, which wanders off and eventually starves. Through all of this, the crane parents never intervene. The surviving chick stays with its parents until it is nine or ten months old, about the time the adults migrate north again for the next breeding season.

Trivia Tidbit

The gray body plumage of the sandhill crane is often tinged with rust. The crane is one of the few birds in the world that actually "paints" its feathers. The crane purposefully dabs its plumage with wads of wet mud. Red iron pigments in the mud stain the bird's feathers a rusty color. The rusty staining makes the adult birds less conspicuous when they are sitting on their nests.

American Coot

Fulica americana

Family Details

Rail Family, 133 species worldwide, 4 prairie species

This large family includes the rails, coots, and gallinules. The behavior of these birds varies so drastically, it's surprising they are related. The rails represent one extreme. Many of the rails are solitary, secretive birds that skulk through dense marsh vegetation under the cover of darkness. They have narrow bodies that they can compress even further to squeeze through vegetation, without a noise or a movement. This characteristic is the origin of the expression "thin as a rail." These traits make rail-watching an exercise in frustration, and on most outings I hear the birds but never see them. For example, in prairie wetlands, I have heard the whistle of the tiny sora rail hundreds of times, yet I have seen the bird only three times.

Coots and gallinules are at the other end of the behavior spectrum. These members of the Rail Family are active during the daytime, gregarious, and highly conspicuous, swimming and diving in open water.

One of the most interesting features of the Rail Family is that over 30 species of rails and gallinules living on islands are flightless, or nearly so. In every case, the islands lack predators. Birds, like all creatures, must balance the energy costs of their behavior with the benefits. Flying takes a great amount of energy, and flight muscles are a heavy burden to carry. On islands where rails no longer needed to escape from predators, it was advantageous for them to become flightless.

Field Identification

From a distance, the coot resembles a small, all-black duck with white feathers under its tail. Notice the chickenlike shape of its white beak and the way the bird bobs its head when it swims. "Mudhen" is one of the coot's nicknames. The coot also has a characteristic way of running across the water's surface for many meters, flapping its wings madly, before it finally becomes airborne.

Where to Find

The hardy, adaptable American coot is common and widespread on sloughs and lakes throughout the prairies.

Wintering Grounds

Prairie coots winter in the southern United States and Mexico. At this time of year, they are highly gregarious, and may gather in large, noisy flocks containing up to 1500 birds. Wintering coots can sometimes become pests, and the surest way for them to do this is to irk a golfer. Coots love to graze on fairways and greens, and their bulky droppings can make putting a challenge. One year in California, tempers flared, and 400 coots were shot by employees of the golf course. More coots were back the next winter.

Diet and Feeding Habits

Coots are mainly vegetarians, and eat the leaves, roots, and seeds of a great variety of aquatic plants. They dive to feed or they upend like a dabbling duck. These birds have long toes fringed with lobes, and strong legs. They can stay underwater for 15 to 20 seconds and may reach depths of 7 meters (23 ft.). Coots also eat insects, snails, and tadpoles.

Breeding Biology

The coot is a prairie bird with a self-important attitude. Pairs aggressively defend their nesting territory against any and all rivals. Intruders are quickly routed in a "splattering-attack," in which the attacker runs, flaps, and splashes noisily across the surface of the water. If the trespasser loiters and is caught by the owner, a fight may ensue. Fighting coots lean back on their tails, grab and slash with their long-clawed feet, and peck each other furiously with their beaks. Coots attack other birds as well, including every variety of prairie duck and grebe. They will even fearlessly chase and tackle a Canada goose that is five times heavier than a coot. Last spring my wife and I spent several weeks photographing ducks from a blind. To our annoyance, the resident coots often drove away our subjects just as they swam within camera range.

Courting male coots arch their wings above their back, flare the white feathers under their tail, and chase the female. The breeding pair builds up to nine floating platforms of cattails and aquatic plants, but they use only one as a nest for their eggs. The extra nests are used for preening, displays, copulation, and brooding their chicks. The average coot nest contains nine speckled, buffy eggs, and both sexes share in the 23- to 27-day incubation. Coot chicks leave the nest soon after hatching. They swim well and paddle along behind their parents, although they sometimes hitch a ride on an adult's back. The young can fly by six weeks of age.

A courting male American coot strikes a handsome pose for a prospective mate.

Immediately after mating, this pair of stilts crossed bills and ran forward together for 5 to 10 meters (16-33 ft.).

Black-necked Stilt

Himantopus mexicanus

Family Details

Avocet and Stilt Family, 7 species worldwide, 2 prairie species.

This is a small family of elegant, slim shorebirds whose bodies are slightly larger than that of a robin, but all have a long, flexible neck and especially long legs. For its size, the black-necked stilt of the prairies has the longest legs of any bird in North America.

The literal translation of the scientific name for the family, *Recurvirostridae*, means "backward curving bill." The stilts have a slightly upturned bill, and that of the avocets is strongly upturned. The stilts and avocets, unlike most shorebirds, nest in loose colonies, and the birds tend to be even more gregarious outside the breeding season. In winter, flocks of several thousand birds may feed together.

Field Identification

The handsome, long-necked stilt is easy to recognize, with its stark black-and-white plumage. The bird has a long, slender, black bill and very long, red legs. At close range, it is possible to see a brownish tinge on the feathers of the female's back; otherwise the sexes are indistinguishable.

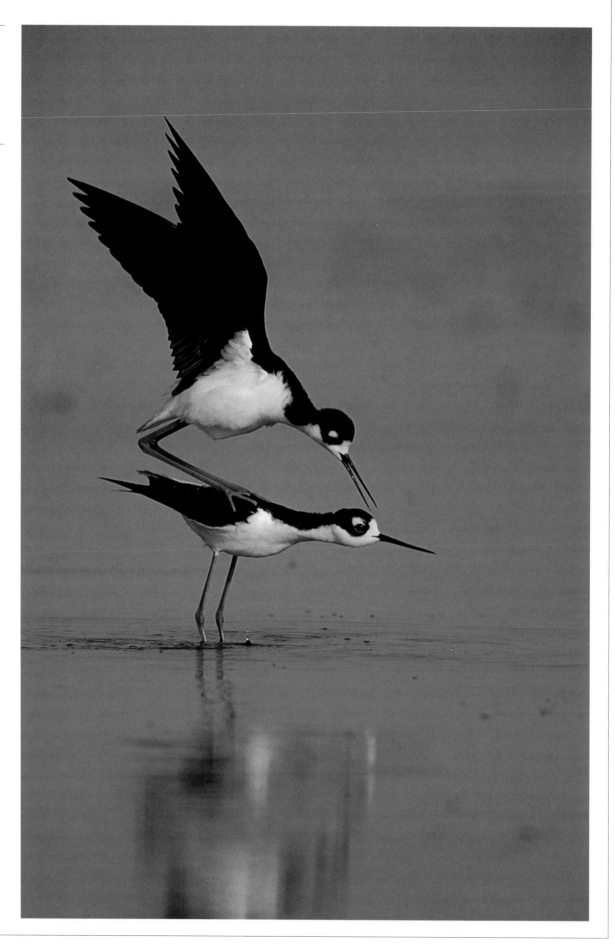

The stilt has proportionately the longest legs of any prairie bird, which makes mating a delicate balancing act.

Where to Find

Until 15 years ago, the black-necked stilt was listed as an erratic visitor and very rare breeder in prairie Alberta. Two nests found in 1977 were attributed to drought conditions, which presumably encouraged the birds to nest farther north than usual. Since that time, stilt numbers have slowly increased, and the bird is now an uncommon breeder in the shallow alkaline sloughs of the southern third of the province. In the spring of 1998, a warm, dry El Niño year, hundreds of stilts were seen in southern Alberta and dozens of nests were reported. The stilt often associates with its close relative the American avocet.

Wintering Grounds

Black-necked stilts are such a recent arrival to the northern prairies that no one has studied them there. The birds likely winter on shallow mudflats along the coasts of Mexico.

Diet and Feeding Habits

The stilt eats mosquito larvae, diving beetles, caddis-flies, mayfly and dragonfly nymphs, grasshoppers, snails, and tiny fish. The bird has unusually strong jaw muscles, and this enables it to rapidly close its beak and firmly grasp small prey. Typically, the black-necked stilt feeds by picking food from the surface and the upper few centimeters of the water column. The stilt and the avocet share the same diet, and the two may lessen competition by simply concentrating on slightly different water depths, the stilt on the surface and the avocet deeper down.

Breeding Biology

The black-necked stilt usually returns to the Canadian prairies in mid-April, and by the end of the month, some pairs are already mating. Stilts nest in small colonies on the ground, and usually build simple mounds of grass stems and twigs hidden in sedges or other short marsh vegetation in shallow water.

The stilt usually lays a clutch of four pale brownish eggs covered with dark spots and blotches. Both sexes share the 24-day incubation. In hot weather, an incubating pair might make more than 100 daily trips to soak their belly feathers in water in order to cool the eggs. New hatchlings look like tiny clumps of down balanced on a pair of toothpicks. Young stilts can run and feed themselves almost from the moment they hatch, but they follow their parents around for about a month, until the youngsters begin to fly.

American Avocet

Recurvirostra americana

Family Details

Avocet and Stilt Family, 7 species worldwide, 2 prairie species

See Black-necked Stilt for a general discussion of the Avocet and Stilt Family.

Field Identification

The avocet is a beautiful shorebird. It has a black and white body, rusty head and neck, and long, bluish gray legs. The female's bill is noticeably shorter and more upturned than the male's; otherwise the sexes are identical.

Where to Find

The American avocet is widespread and common on shallow sloughs and marshes throughout the prairies. The bird is often associated with alkaline wetlands and the mudflats of shallow lakes and irrigation ponds.

Wintering Grounds

Most avocets spend the winter on intertidal mudflats, brackish-water ponds, and impoundments along the Pacific or Atlantic coasts of Mexico and Central America. Like most shorebirds, they migrate south before the end of summer, with the peak exodus occurring in late August.

Diet and Feeding Habits

The inside of an avocet's bill is fringed, and the bird uses this to filter minute food items from the water. The most common foods include snails, aquatic beetles, dragonfly nymphs, water boatmen, midges, and water fleas, but they also eat some seeds and small bits of water plants. In alkaline sloughs, avocets eat large numbers of brine shrimp and brine flies. The classic way for an avocet to feed is to sweep its bill back and forth through the water, wielding its beak as if it were a scythe. The birds also pick food off the surface, and submerge their heads to capture underwater prey.

Breeding Biology

Avocets usually form pairs on their wintering grounds or during their spring migration. Soon after they return to the prairies in late April, the pairs stake out and defend small feeding territories. These territories may or may not be close to their eventual nest site. Both the male and the female will drive away other avocets.

Avocets nest in small, loose colonies along shorelines, or on islands, which afford them more protection from predators. In early May 1998, I spent dozens of hours watching avocets. I saw their elaborate mating ritual many times and described it in my journal: "It is early evening, and a pair of avocets is very close to my blind, their elegant bodies perfectly reflected in the smooth blue water of the slough. Suddenly the female bows forward and stretches her neck low down, just above the surface of the water. She stays frozen in this pose. I can tell it is the female by the greater curve in her beak. Her mate begins to preen vigorously, dipping his bill in the water and splashing the female in the process. The male walks excitedly from one side of the female to the other, the intensity of his preening and water splashing increasing with every moment. After six or seven changes in

position, the male jumps onto the female's back, fluttering his wings to keep his balance. For an instant their cloacas 'kiss,' then the male slides off and the pair run together through the water for a dozen steps, their necks entwined in a gentle embrace."

Avocets build a simple nest of grass and twigs on the ground. I have found many nests, and they were always in the open. The cryptically colored, pear-shaped eggs, usually four of them, blend well with the surroundings and make the nest very difficult to locate. Both sexes take turns incubating the eggs for the 23-day period. The birds alternate frequently throughout the day, changing places every 40 to 80 minutes. In hot weather, the incubating parents soak their belly feathers in water before sitting on the nest. This cools the eggs and keeps the nest humidity high. The chicks are able to leave the nest within two hours of hatching, and they stay with their parents until they are four weeks old and have begun to fly.

An avocet drives a rival from its feeding territory in the shallow water of a slough.

64

Wilson's Phalarope

Phalaropus tricolor

Family Details

Snipe, Sandpiper, and Phalarope Family, 86 species worldwide, 20 prairie species

The common name for this family of small- to medium-sized birds is shorebirds. Although all of them swim well, and walk and run with ease on dry land, they are best known for their habit of wading and feeding in shallow water along beaches and coastlines. Most of the family members are rather plainly colored in buff, grays, and browns, but they vary greatly in size from the sparrow-sized sand-pipers, called "peeps," to the crow-sized godwits and curlews. With the exception of the phalaropes, male and female birds in this family are quite similar in appearance.

Shorebirds display a great variety of bill sizes and shapes. This diversity enables them to exploit a wider range of foods, and lessens the competition among them. Within the family, there are sandpipers with slender, pointed bills that rapidly probe the mud like the needle on a sewing machine, needle-nosed phalaropes that deftly pick minute plankton from the water's surface, flat-beaked turnstones that flip over pebbles to uncover hidden prey, godwits with long, upturned bills, and whimbrels with bills that curve downward. Most of these birds have bill tips that are densely covered with sensitive touch receptors, which allow the owner to detect food buried deep in the mud. Through a remarkable feat of engineering, a shorebird is able to open just the tip of its bill while the rest remains closed. The bone inside the upper part of the beak slides forward, causing the tip to bend upward. The bird then pinches the prey in the movable tip.

Field Identification

Wilson's phalarope is a small shorebird with a needle-like beak. The bird feeds on the water's sur-face, and often spins like a top. The female phalarope is larger and more brightly colored than the male. She has a bold black stripe on the side of her face and neck, rust and gray back and wings, and a white belly. The male is similarly patterned, but duller in tone.

In phalaropes, the sexual roles are reversed. The drab male Wilson's phalarope incubates the eggs and cares for the chicks.

Where to Find

The phalarope is found throughout the prairies in soggy ditches, shallow sloughs, and sedge wetlands.

Wintering Grounds

The phalarope is one of the few shorebirds that migrates to an area specifically to molt at the end of the breeding season. Females begin to leave the prairie breeding areas as early as mid-June. The males follow several weeks later, and juveniles are the last to leave. They all gather on large alkaline lakes such as Old Wives Lake and Chaplin Lake in Saskatchewan, Abert Lake in Oregon, and Mono Lake in California. Over 600,000 Wilson's phalaropes may gather at the Great Salt Lake in Utah. In these alkaline lakes, the birds molt and fatten in preparation for the rigors of their long southward migration. The autumn migration begins in late July and occurs throughout August. Most Wilson's phalaropes fly to alkaline lakes in the high Andes of Bolivia, Argentina, and Chile. They make this exhausting 5500-kilometer (3400-mi.) journey in a single, nonstop flight lasting 54 hours or more.

Diet and Feeding Habits

Phalaropes eat all the usual small aquatic invertebrates: beetles, fly larvae, snails, water boatmen, and damselfly nymphs. On alkaline lakes, they commonly gorge on brine shrimps and brine flies until their bodies are padded in fat. The phalarope often uses a distinctive feeding technique called "spinning." I wrote about it in *A is for Arctic: Natural Wonders of a Polar World*: "… like a whirling dervish, a hungry phalarope spins rapidly around in a tight circle on the surface of the water. The spinning produces a miniature whirlpool that funnels insects and small aquatic invertebrates toward the surface, where they are stabbed by the pirouetting predator."

Phalaropes may also follow wading avocets to feed on any tiny animals that are stirred up by the birds' feet. In the high Andes of northern Chile, at an altitude of 4400 meters (14,400 ft.), I watched phalaropes follow Andean and James flamingos for exactly the same reason.

Breeding Biology

In general, shorebirds show the greatest variety of mating systems of any group of birds. Some species are monogamous, many are promiscuous. In some cases, males breed in sequence or simultaneously with several females in a single season; in other instances, the female raises several families, each fathered by a different male. The phalaropes, however, carry the avian sexual revolution one step further: in these birds, the sexes have completely reversed their roles. Female Wilson's phalaropes are more brightly colored and larger than the males. Up to 10 aggressive females may court and follow a single harried male in an aerial chase. To win a mate, the females may even fight each other with flapping wings and stabbing beaks. A successful female "jealously" guards her partner. Under her watchful eye, the male builds a nest of fine grasses on the ground, and once the eggs are laid he alone incubates them. The female phalarope deserts her partner soon after he begins to incubate. She may then try to mate with a second partner or simply migrate to the molting area. Meanwhile, the male phalarope incubates the eggs for about three weeks, and stays with the chicks for another three weeks afterwards. During this time he leads them from one feeding area to the next, broods them when it is cold, and warns them when a predator appears.

Long-billed Curlew

Numenius americanus

Family Details

Snipe, Sandpiper, and Phalarope Family, 86 species worldwide, 20 prairie species

See Wilson's Phalarope for a general discussion of the Snipe, Sandpiper, and Phalarope Family.

Field Identification

The crow-sized long-billed curlew has a wingspan up to 100 centimeters (39 in.), making it the largest shorebird in North America. The curlew is mottled brown in color, but in flight, its cinnamon-colored

Young curlews, like most nestling shorebirds, are cryptically marked and rely on camouflage to hide them from predators.

"armpits" are clearly visible and distinguish it from most other large shorebirds. As its name suggests, the bird's 23-centimeter (9-in.) curved bill is its most distinctive feature. Female curlews are larger than their mates and have an appreciably longer bill. The typical call of the curlew is a loud, plaintive *cur-lew*, usually repeated.

Where to Find
The curlew is an uncommon resident of the dry shortgrass prairies. In Canada, the species has been slowly declining over the last 30 years and is currently listed as vulnerable. The gradual plowing and cultivation of native grasslands is the main reason for the decline.

Wintering Grounds
The long-billed curlew winters on mudflats and beaches from California and Texas south to Guatemala. The birds migrate south in August and return to the prairies in early April.

Diet and Feeding Habits
A foraging long-billed curlew seems very much out of place as it walks purposefully across the dry prairies, pecking here and there for grasshoppers, crickets, caterpillars, and nestling songbirds. A feeding bird is in constant motion as it zigzags across the prairie, wielding its extraordinary bill more deftly than a surgeon with a pair of long-handled forceps.

On the wintering grounds, the curlew uses its long bill to probe tidal flats for lugworms, ragworms, and clams buried deep in the mud.

Breeding Biology
An adult long-billed curlew may not begin to breed until it is three years old. Often, the birds are already paired when they arrive on the breeding grounds. Unpaired males immediately begin to perform conspicuous gliding displays, floating over the flat prairies, calling loudly to advertise their availability, as well as their vigor and health.

Curlews, in common with all shorebirds, lay four pear-shaped eggs that fit perfectly together. The nest consists of a shallow scrape on the ground, scantily lined with fine grasses. Even with the nest being out in the open prairie, the heavily speckled, buff-colored eggs are very hard to see. The cryptic coloration of the adults also makes the nest difficult for predators to locate. I once crawled slowly within a few meters of an incubating curlew to examine the fine pattern and color of its plumage. There is nothing quite as exciting as being within a few arms'-lengths of a wild creature, with the soft wind of the prairie stroking your cheek and the fragrant aroma of grass and sun-heated sage filling your nostrils. The curlew stayed perfectly still, its neck stretched along the ground, and it remained that way as I slowly backed away, my heart pounding with excitement.

Both sexes incubate the eggs until they hatch at

The long-billed curlew's 23-centimeter (9-in.) beak is the bird's most distinctive feature.

28 days. Commonly, the eggs hatch within five hours of each other, and the downy chicks leave the nest within a day. From the beginning, young curlew chicks feed themselves, but they are brooded by both parents whenever they become cold or bad weather threatens. The female usually abandons her brood when they are just two to three weeks old, and the male continues to guard them until they fledge, at six weeks of age.

Willet

Catoptrophorus semipalmatus

Family Details
Snipe, Sandpiper, and Phalarope Family,
86 species worldwide, 20 prairie species

See Wilson's Phalarope for a general discussion of the Snipe, Sandpiper, and Phalarope Family.

Field Identification
The willet is a grayish, medium-sized sandpiper that looks rather plain when loafing on the shoreline or wading in the shallows. In flight, however, the bird flaunts its white rump and striking black and white

wings. The unmistakable "flashing" wing pattern is visible from a great distance and undoubtedly functions as a signal for other birds.

Where to Find
The willet is one of the most common shorebirds in the prairies. This unwary, noisy sandpiper frequents sloughs, irrigation ponds, wet meadows, and ditches. Sometimes the first clue to the willet's presence is the distinctive sound of its loud call, in which it repeatedly sings its name.

Wintering Grounds
Willets spend the winter along the southern Pacific and Atlantic coasts of the United States. I remember photographing these birds on the muddy tidal flats of southern Florida. When a whole flock took flight, their flashing black and white wings produced a dazzling effect.

Diet and Feeding Habits
The willet has a stout beak for its size, and it eats the large aquatic invertebrates that lurk in the mud and water of the slough: worms, snails, beetles, dragonfly nymphs, small fish, and leeches. Last spring, I was surprised when a willet grabbed a large predatory water beetle that seemed to be half the size of the bird's head. The beetle was gone in a gulp.

After a bout of preening, many birds stretch their wings—as this willet is doing—to settle their plumage.

Breeding Biology

Willets are highly aggressive birds, and the males defend their territory with a conspicuous flight display during which they fly in circles with their wings arched downward, flapping them in short rapid beats. The wing action creates a flickering pattern. Some males climb so high that they are almost out of sight.

Willet nests are usually well hidden in heavy grasses, and are generally located near water. On occasion I have found their nests far out on the dry prairie, with no water in sight. The birds normally lay four eggs, with the female doing most of the incubation, though the male may take over at night. The precocious chicks leave the nest as soon as they hatch. In late spring, when temperatures can be cool, young, downy willets scurry around the prairie pecking and probing until they slowly become chilled. Their movements gradually slow down as their body temperature drops from its normal 40°C (104°F) to 31 or 32°C (88–90°F). When this happens, they huddle under a parent, quickly warm up, and off they go again. Author Dr. Paul Johnsgard reported, in *The Plovers, Sandpipers, and Snipes of the World*, an adult willet carrying each of its four newly hatched chicks between its thighs across several creeks and over a marshland for a distance of half a kilometer (0.3 mi.).

The female adult abandons her chicks after several weeks, leaving the male to care for the young. The male may also abandon the chicks before they fledge, but this aspect of the willet's life has not been well studied.

Upland Sandpiper
Bartramia longicauda

Family Details

Snipe, Sandpiper, and Phalarope Family, 86 species worldwide, 20 prairie species

See Wilson's Phalarope for a general discussion of the Snipe, Sandpiper, and Phalarope Family.

Field Identification

The upland sandpiper has a relatively small head, a long neck and tail, and bright yellow legs and beak. This medium-sized sandpiper often lands on fenceposts, telephone poles, and large boulders. When it alights, it frequently holds its wings extended above its back for a moment or two before folding them.

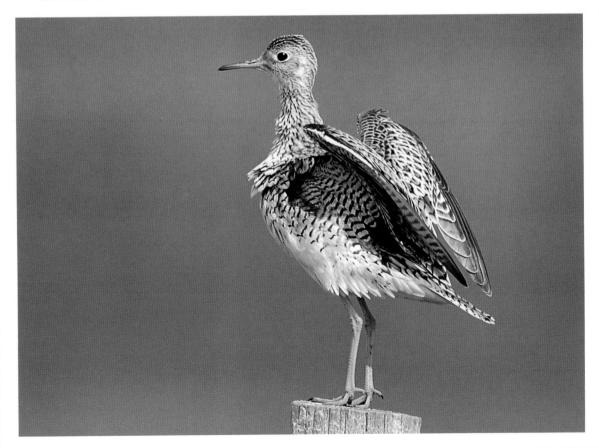

The upland sandpiper favors native grasslands and does not adapt well to agriculture.

Where to Find

At the turn of the century, the upland sandpiper was much more widespread than it is today, and was one of the most common birds on the prairies. Today, this pretty sandpiper occurs in localized patches throughout the prairies wherever native grasslands have been spared from the plow. The upland sandpiper, unlike most prairie shorebirds, is rarely found near water. As its name suggests, the bird prefers pastures, rangelands, and dry, rolling prairies.

Wintering Grounds

The upland sandpiper, like so many shorebirds, is a long-distance migrant that flees to the warmer climes of South America in late summer, well before the first icy winds of autumn sweep down across the prairies. Most of these birds winter in the grasslands of southern Brazil, and in northern and central Argentina. By April, these delightful songsters are back again enlivening the skies over native grasslands.

Diet and Feeding Habits

The upland sandpiper is a sprint-and-peck predator, sprinting here and there to catch grasshoppers, weevils, and crickets. It also eats caterpillars, beetles, ants, moths, flies, spiders, snails, bugs, centipedes, millipedes, and earthworms—essentially anything that wiggles, creeps, scuttles, and flutters.

Breeding Biology

The male upland sandpiper, in common with many birds living on the flat, treeless prairies, sings on the wing while circling high in the sky. The bird's drawn-out whistle reminds me of the "wolf" whistle my friends and I used as teenagers when we wanted to flirt with a girl. The whistle is more effective for the male sandpiper than it was for me.

Most sandpipers are already paired when they return to the prairies in spring, and the partners quickly claim a territory and whistle the news to the neighbors. Within two weeks of arrival, most of the pairs have begun to nest. In a North Dakota study, 183 out of 199 nests were located in native prairie. Some prairie shorebirds, such as curlews, willets, and godwits, have adapted somewhat to agricultural land and they sometimes nest in stubble fields; the upland sandpiper never has, and when the native prairie disappears, so will it.

A tuft of overhanging grass often hides the sandpiper's nest, which is usually a simple hollow on the ground lined with small twigs, leaves, and grasses. The usual clutch of four glossy, speckled eggs is incubated for three weeks, the duties shared by both partners. Within a day of hatching, young sandpiper chicks leave the nest and follow their parents, who continue to brood them and alert them to danger for a month afterwards.

Trivia Tidbit

In the 1880s, when passenger pigeon numbers began to decline from overhunting, the market gunners shifted their sights to upland sandpipers. Great numbers of these prairie birds were slaughtered during their spring migration when they passed overhead in enormous flocks. Eventually the hunting stopped, and the sandpipers began a slow recovery, but never regained their former abundance. Today, the steady loss of native grasslands threatens to reduce their numbers once again. In prairie Canada, the upland sandpiper has been declining by 2 percent every year for the last 30 years.

Marbled Godwit

Limosa fedoa

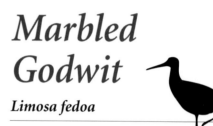

Family Details

Snipe, Sandpiper, and Phalarope Family, 86 species worldwide, 20 prairie species

See Wilson's Phalarope for a general discussion of the Snipe, Sandpiper, and Phalarope Family.

Field Identification

The marbled godwit, with a wingspan of 80 centimeters (32 in.), is one of the largest prairie shorebirds, second only to the long-billed curlew. The godwit is mottled brown in color with conspicuous cinnamon linings on the undersides of its wings. The bird has a long, upturned bill with a pink base, which distinguishes it from the curlew, whose bill curves strongly downward.

Where to Find

The godwit is a bird of the northern Great Plains, being found in shortgrass prairies, flooded fields, alkaline lakes, and sloughs. In the best wetland habitats, there may be three pairs of nesting godwits per square kilometer (0.4 sq. mi.).

Wintering Grounds

Most prairie godwits winter on the mud flats, beaches, and associated wetlands of the southern Pacific and Atlantic coasts of the United States. A few birds may migrate as far as Central America.

Diet and Feeding Habits

When the godwit feeds on dry uplands, it concentrates on grasshoppers and beetles, probing tufts of vegetation for insects hidden in the greenery. In water, the bird wades to the top of its thighs and often submerges its head to probe deep into the mud with its 13-centimeter (5-in.) bill. The godwit "feels" for leeches, worms, and insect larvae using the rich network of sensors at the tip of its beak. Because it does not use vision to locate most of its food, the godwit can also feed at night.

Breeding Biology

The marbled godwit returns to the prairies in early May. Last spring while I was photographing avocets from a blind, I watched an energetic male godwit repeatedly perform his aerial display, called a ceremonial flight, over the edge of the slough where I was hiding. I described the performance in my journal: "This is the fourth day in a row that I have watched the godwit wheel and sing over the prairie. The bird usually climbs to an altitude of about 50 meters (164 ft.) and slowly circles while calling loudly. The rich cinnamon of his underwings flashes brightly in the warmth of the late afternoon sun. At the end of his circular glide, he sometimes folds his wings and plummets towards the ground in a power dive, only to brake at the last moment and land softly. In a final display, the grounded godwit momentarily holds his rusty wings aloft as if he were saluting his own aerial achievement. His mastery of flight is a delight to watch."

The marbled godwit usually nests on the ground on the open prairie, sometimes quite far from the water. It may also nest in small, loose colonies, with three or four nests clustered within several hundred square meters. The birds lay four glossy olive-brown eggs patterned with scrawls and small blotches. Both parents share the three-week incubation, and afterwards stay with the chicks for up to a month until they finally fledge.

Killdeer

Charadrius vociferus

Family Details

Plover Family, 67 species worldwide, 6 prairie species

This family includes the plovers and lapwings. This second group of shorebirds is closely related to the snipes, sandpipers, and phalaropes. Unlike the sandpipers, which display a wide range of body sizes and beak shapes, the plovers are rather uniform in size and have a relatively short, blunt bill that is swollen near the tip.

The big-eyed plovers hunt by sight and pick their prey from the surface of the ground, unlike sandpipers, which probe the mud and feel for their food.

Many plovers have conspicuous black bands on their heads and breasts, and their plumage is often a bold mix of brown, olive, gray, black, and white, quite different from the plain, mottled-brown feathers so common among the snipes and sandpipers. Even though plovers are boldly patterned, the black bands on their bodies break up their silhouette and help them blend in with their surroundings. Male and female plovers are similar in appearance.

Field Identification

The killdeer is roughly the size of a robin, and is the most common plover on the prairies. The two black bands across the bird's white neck and breast distinguish it from all other species, and in flight, its rusty-colored rump is distinct. At close range, the killdeer has a narrow, bright orange ring around its eyes.

The bird's common name is an imitation of its call, *kill-dee, kill-dee*, and its scientific name, *vociferus*, reflects how loud and noisy it can be.

Where to Find

The killdeer is widespread throughout the prairies. As you might expect, the bird is a frequent visitor to sloughs, irrigation ponds, and wet pastures, but the adaptable plover is also common in cultivated fields, golf courses, airports, the gravel shoulders of roadways, and dry prairies far from water.

Wintering Grounds

Killdeers winter in coastal regions from southern British Columbia all the way to northern South America. On their wintering grounds, the birds may forage alone, or in loose flocks of up to 50 birds. The killdeer is often one of the earliest spring migrants to return to the prairies. In March, when snow patches still cover the ground, the bird's noisy calls are a welcome reminder that spring is on its way.

The killdeer is one of the earliest migrants to return to the northern prairies in spring.

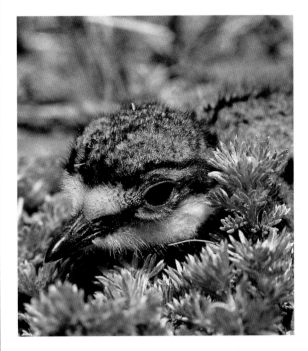

predator than are the eggs, so the parent birds take fewer risks to protect the chicks, and their distraction displays are less daring as time goes on. Hatchling killdeers forage with their parents until they begin to fly at around four weeks of age. After the first set of chicks becomes independent, some adult killdeers may raise a second brood.

Piping Plover
Charadrius melodus

Family Details
Plover Family, 67 species worldwide, 6 prairie species
See Killdeer for a general discussion of the Plover Family.

Field Identification
The piping plover is a small, pale shorebird, with a white face, neck, and belly, sandy wings and back, and orange legs. The bird has a single black band across its forehead and another around its neck.

Where to Find
This attractive plover is the most endangered shorebird in North America, with fewer than 2300 breeding pairs in Canada and the United States. Slightly more than half of the birds breed in the northern Great Plains, from the southern Prairie provinces south to Nebraska. Many of the plovers in this area are found along the shores of large alkaline lakes, such as Big Quill Lake and Chaplin Lake in Saskatchewan, and Chain of Lakes in North Dakota.

Wintering Grounds
The piping plover winters on mud flats and sand beaches scattered along the Gulf of Mexico. For example, one bird that was banded at Handhills Lake, Alberta, wintered three years in a row on Marco Island on the Gulf Coast of Florida. Most piping plovers leave the prairies by early August, and return again in April.

Diet and Feeding Habits
The piping plover is closely tied to the shoreline, and generally feeds within 5 meters (16 ft.) of the water's edge. One North Dakota study revealed that the birds spent 42 percent of their time foraging at the waterline, and 45 percent of their time searching the gravel areas on the beach nearby.

The piping plover, as well as a number of other plovers, uses an intriguing feeding technique called

Diet and Feeding Habits
Throughout the year, the killdeer feeds primarily on insects, and is especially skilled at capturing beetles and grasshoppers. The stomachs of some individuals may contain hundreds of weevils and grasshoppers, both of which are serious agricultural pests. The killdeer hunts in the usual plover manner of sprinting for a meter or two, freezing, then pecking the prey off the ground.

Breeding Biology
In the late 1950s, the birdwatching craze was still decades away. Then, as a 10-year-old boy, I liked to wander alone in the woods and fields of my uncle's dairy farm in southern Ontario and search for birds. The killdeer's was the first bird's nest I ever found. I still remember my excitement at finding the four speckled eggs resting in a hollow, in the gravel, at the edge of the road. When I accidentally flushed the adult bird from the nest, it flapped along the ground, dragging its wings, flaring its tail, and exposing its bright rusty rump. I thought for a moment that I had stepped on the bird and injured it. The killdeer, in common with many shorebirds, is an accomplished actor, and its "broken-wing display" is used to distract coyotes, foxes, and other predators and lure them away from its nest. Both the male and the female killdeer perform distraction displays, and the displays tend to be most daring just before the eggs hatch at the end of the 25-day incubation period. The parents, at this point, have invested a great amount of time, and have the most to lose if the eggs are predated. Once the chicks hatch, they scatter and crouch in the grass whenever danger threatens. Young killdeers are less likely to be detected by a

"foot trembling." While standing still, the bird stretches a leg forward and rapidly stomps on the wet mud with its foot. Researchers believe this behavior may mimic the vibration of waves, fooling invertebrates buried in the mud into moving and exposing their location.

The plover eats any small invertebrate found on the beach: worms, midges, beetles, spiders, grasshoppers, and snails. At Reflex Lake in eastern Alberta,

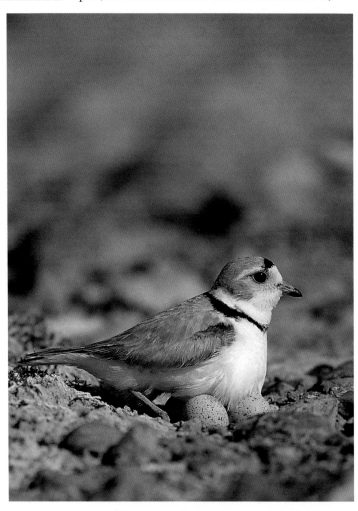

A clutch of four piping plover eggs weighs almost as much as the adult bird.

I watched fast-moving plovers run and snatch brine flies that were swarming along the water's edge. The birds fed alongside large flocks of migrating sanderlings and black-bellied plovers, all of whom were gorging on the abundance of insects.

Breeding Biology

Beginning in late April, male piping plovers each defend a small territory that includes a section of shoreline for foraging, and an adjacent section of gravelly beach for nesting. In North Dakota, where they were studied, the nests were sometimes as close as 14 meters (46 ft.) apart, but more often the distance was three times that. The plovers may use noth-

ing more than a shallow scrape in the sand to cradle their four tan, speckled eggs. However, on gravel shorelines, the birds often line their nests with tiny pebbles, and generally continue to add pebbles throughout laying and incubation.

The chicks hatch after 28 days, and typical of all shorebirds, the downy youngsters can run, hide, and feed themselves within a day or two. Some adult females desert their brood after only five to ten days, but in many cases, both parents stay with the chicks even after they fledge, and sometimes until the start of migration in August.

The prairie piping plover is in serious trouble for several reasons. When water levels drop in prairie lakes, because of drought or excessive drainage for agriculture, grasses and other plants quickly invade the dry shorelines. When this happens, the shoreline is no longer suitable for nesting, and the plovers abandon the lake even if there is still an abundance of food.

Rising water levels in some lakes also pose a threat to nesting piping plovers. The best example of this is Lake Diefenbaker in southern Saskatchewan. This large reservoir supports the highest number of piping plovers in North America, perhaps 10 percent of the world population. Typically, the reservoir is filled in late May, just after the plovers have finished laying their eggs, and most of the nests are lost to flooding.

Disturbance by livestock is yet another problem for plovers on the prairies. In one study in Saskatchewan, grazing cattle were identified as the greatest threat to the plovers on 21 lakes.

Probably the number one cause of breeding failure in prairie plovers is predation. In various years predators have destroyed 40 percent of the plover nests in Manitoba, 72 percent in Saskatchewan, and 93 percent in North Dakota. The common culprits are red foxes, striped skunks, American crows, herring gulls, California gulls, and ring-billed gulls. In recent decades, these gulls have greatly increased in numbers, mainly because of their ability to scavenge off humans. More gulls equals more pressure on nesting plovers. To counteract this threat, biologists in some areas now erect heavy fences over plover nests to protect them from predators, as well as from trampling by cattle, and as a result, hatching success has increased dramatically, sometimes exceeding 80 percent.

Despite the attention the piping plover has received, it is still too little, too late, and plover numbers continue to decline. Some authorities predict the bird may be gone from the prairies before the end of the next century. That would be an embarrassing tragedy.

California Gull

Larus californicus

Family Details

Gull Family, 51 species worldwide, 3 prairie species

The familiar gulls are a family of heavy-bodied, medium-sized to large seabirds. All have long, narrow, pointed wings, webbed feet, and a stout, hooked bill. The adaptable gulls will eat almost anything they can swallow, and many are accomplished scavengers. This flexibility has enabled the family to inhabit every continent, and they occupy a greater range of latitudes (84° North to 68° South) than any other group of birds on earth.

The gulls are seabirds, and indeed most species are found primarily in coastal regions, although some species occur far inland. The three gulls in the prairies, for example, have large breeding ranges in the center of the continent.

Field Identification

The California gull is a medium-sized gull with a white head and neck, gray back, gray wings with black wingtips, and yellow legs. It differs from the ring-billed gull by having dark brown eyes, and its yellow bill has red and black spots on the tip. Adult male and female Californias, as in all gulls, are similar in appearance.

It takes four years for a California gull to acquire its full adult appearance, and therefore a young gull can be a huge challenge to identify. In its first summer, a juvenile is all brown with black legs and a pink bill tipped with black. As it ages, the color of its legs changes from black to pink, to gray, only to end up yellow. As well, white feathers appear in the plumage gradually, giving the bird a mottled appearance until eventually it turns a solid white and gray.

A parent California gull must guard its chicks from neighboring adults who will cannibalize them if given a chance.

The black pigment melanin makes the wingtips of the California gull resistant to wear and abrasion.

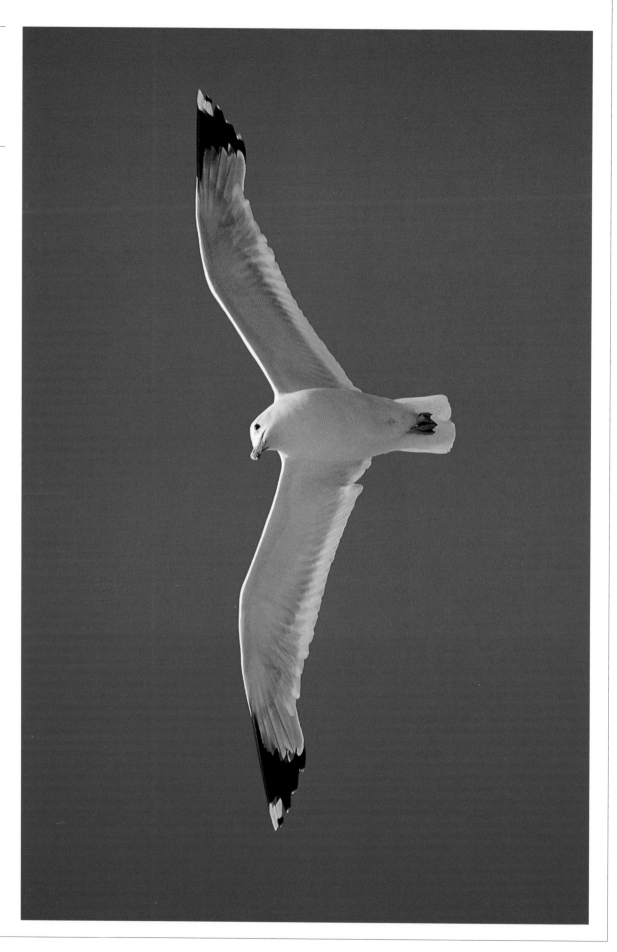

Where to Find

The breeding range of the California gull is concentrated in the northern Great Plains, where there are roughly 200 colonies of these gregarious seabirds. Alberta has the greatest number of colonies, with 50, 6 of which contain over 20,000 birds each. Saskatchewan ranks second, with 21 colonies. Both Montana and Utah have 19 colonies. Throughout their range the gulls frequent large sloughs, lakes, reservoirs, farmlands, and garbage dumps.

Wintering Grounds

Most California gulls winter along the Pacific Coast from Washington State to northern Mexico. The gulls are unusual because they continually change locations throughout the autumn, winter, and spring. Rather than restrict themselves to a single wintering site, the birds slowly wander over a huge wintering range.

Diet and Feeding Habits

The California gull, like many other gulls, is very resourceful at finding food. In irrigated fields, it waits for voles and pocket gophers to be flooded out of their burrows. The gulls follow plows to feed on exposed insects and earthworms, and in croplands they feed on great numbers of grasshoppers. The gulls' prodigious appetite for grasshoppers earned them a large gilded statue, which was erected by early Mormons in Salt Lake City, Utah, to commemorate the birds' role in ridding crops of these plant-munching insects.

California gulls often share nesting islands with ring-billed gulls and double-crested cormorants, and they readily gobble up any unattended eggs and small chicks belonging to these species. Californias will also cannibalize their own kind, and eat the eggs and chicks of any inattentive neighbors. In fact, chicks up to 40 days old are very vulnerable, and may be attacked and killed any time they wander out of their parents' protective territory.

Breeding Biology

California gulls often return to the prairies by the end of March. One year, I hiked out to an island colony in a slough that was still capped by 20 centimeters (8 in.) of ice. The island was covered with snow, and the gulls had already begun setting up their nesting territories.

The gulls lay two or three blotched olive-green eggs in a simple ground nest made of discarded feathers and dried bird bones left from previous nesting seasons. Gull parents build their nest together, and both sexes incubate the eggs, taking shifts of three to four hours, which gives the off-duty bird enough time to forage. The downy, salt-and-pepper-patterned chicks are fed regurgitated food by both adults until they fledge at about six weeks of age.

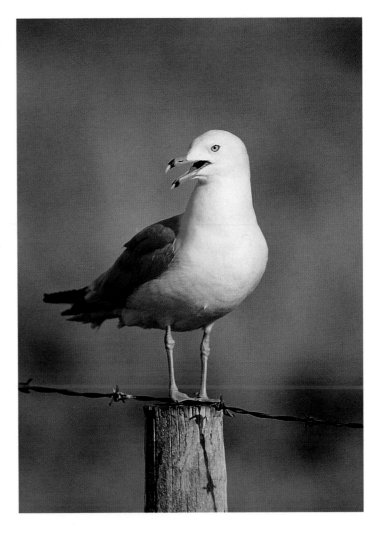

Ring-billed Gull

Larus delawarensis

Family Details

Gull Family, 51 species worldwide, 3 prairie species

See California Gull for a general discussion of the Gull Family.

Field Identification

The ring-billed gull is smaller than the California gull, but very similar in appearance. Both have white heads and black wingtips, and from a distance may be difficult to distinguish. If you get close enough you will notice that the ring-billed gull has pale yellow eyes, and its bright yellow bill has a black band near the tip.

Ring-bills take three years to acquire their full adult appearance. The juveniles are mottled brown, with dark eyes, a dark beak, and gray legs. As they

No self-respecting birdwatcher would slur the ring-billed gull, or any other gull species, by calling it a seagull.

mature, their eyes, beak, and legs lighten in color, the mottling gradually disappears, and their dark feathers are replaced with white and gray ones.

Where to Find
The ring-billed gull is widespread and common throughout the prairies and is found in sloughs, cultivated fields, and irrigated croplands.

Wintering Grounds
The ring-bill winters in the southern United States on inland lakes and waterways, and along the coasts. This gull is extremely gregarious; as many as 50,000 birds may gather at a single landfill. The gulls migrate south in October and are among the last birds to leave the prairies in autumn. They migrate north again in early April.

Diet and Feeding Habits
The ring-bill frequently forages in fields, especially in the spring after the land has been freshly plowed. Its most important food is earthworms, but it also eats insects, meadow voles, deer mice, and waste grain. One of its favorite hangouts is the parking lot of fast-food restaurants, where it scavenges garbage and begs for food scraps. When I see these birds scrounging around my favorite hamburger outlets, I am reassured that the food is at least marginally edible. Having said that, ring-bills seem to have an iron-coated digestive tract, and perhaps I should reevaluate them as food critics.

Breeding Biology
These birds are just as gregarious on their breeding grounds as they are on their wintering grounds. In the prairies, hundreds and even thousands of birds may gather at a single nesting colony. Around the Great Lakes, there are immense ring-bill colonies, some containing up to 80,000 nesting pairs! Most colonies are located on islands, which greatly lessens the risk from egg-napping coyotes, red foxes, and striped skunks. A marauding skunk, for example, may destroy 30 to 40 nests in a single night raid. The total damage, however, may be much greater than this since many eggs are broken when the startled gulls fly off in panic. As well, other eggs are lost when they become excessively cooled because the frightened adults delay returning to their nests.

Ring-bills lay one to three olive-gray eggs that are heavily marked with dark splotches. The nest is a sparse collection of twigs, small sticks, grasses, and leaves piled on the ground. Both sexes build the nest and share in the incubation duties. Dense colonies may have two or three nests in every square meter (9 sq. ft.), and the neighbors bicker continuously. If an egg accidentally rolls out of the nest during an argu-

If a Franklin's gull leaves its nest for any length of time the neighbors will quickly dismantle it.

ment, the owner will retrieve it. This behavior is instinctive, and sometimes the birds get their wires crossed. In one Oregon colony, 4 percent of the nests contained egg-size pebbles, which the gulls probably mistook for errant eggs.

Nestling gull chicks are covered with down, their eyes are open, and they can walk around clumsily within a day or two of hatching. Even so, they are not self-sufficient like the precocious chicks of the grouse and shorebird families, and must be fed by their parents. The chicks recognize the unique sound of their parents' voices by the time they are four or five days old. Young ring-bills make their first flights when they are five weeks old, and the family breaks up sometime afterwards.

Franklin's Gull
Larus pipixcan

Family Details
Gull Family, 51 species worldwide,
3 prairie species

See California Gull for a general discussion of the Gull Family.

Field Identification
The Franklin's gull is easy to identify since it is the only gull in the prairies with a black head. Early in the breeding season, the bird's breast and belly feathers are suffused with a delicate pink hue. Because of

this subtle coloration, the naturalist on the Franklin Expedition of 1823 named it Franklin's rosy gull.

The Franklin's gull takes two years to reach full adult plumage. Even so, juveniles at the end of their first summer still look a lot like their parents.

Where to Find
The Franklin's gull nests on large marshes and sloughs throughout the northern Great Plains. At the end of the breeding season in the last half of July, the birds desert their nesting grounds and wander widely over the prairies for the rest of the summer, foraging in flooded fields, croplands, and native grasslands.

Wintering Grounds
The gulls leave the northern prairies in September, and migrate to the western coast of Peru and northern Chile. The 14,000-kilometer (8700-mi.) round-trip migration is one of the longest trips made by any gull. En route, the gulls may gather in huge flocks. One November, an estimated 750,000 birds were recorded on Lake Texona, Texas, and one October, a phenomenal 2.5 million Franklin's gulls darkened the skies above Salt Plains National Wildlife Refuge in Oklahoma.

Diet and Feeding Habits
Near its nesting colony, the Franklin's gull swoops for midges that swarm above the slough, and it also picks insects and aquatic invertebrates off the surface of the water. On the prairies, flocks of hungry Franklin's gulls follow the plow, diving through the dust to feed on grasshoppers, beetles, caterpillars, fly larvae, and earthworms.

Breeding Biology
These gulls nest in colonies with as few as 25 pairs, but usually their colonies are larger. Some very large colonies may include 100,000 nests, scattered among the cattails of a marsh. The location of these nests is hardly a secret as hundreds or thousands of birds scream and circle above the marsh. Their floating nest mound is made of cattails and bulrushes, the same kind favored by the American coot. Squabbling between the two species can be quite intense, and the coot usually wins. The nesting gulls relentlessly compete with each other as well. If a pair is careless enough to leave their nest unguarded for an hour or more, the nest will likely be completely dismantled and stolen by the neighbors.

The gulls usually lay three olive-green eggs, speckled and scrawled with brown, black, and gray. Like all gulls, both parents incubate and feed the young, which stay on the nest mound until they are about three weeks old. The young gulls begin to fly when they are five weeks old, and the family breaks up a week or two later.

Forster's Tern
Sterna forsteri

Family Details
Tern Family, 44 species worldwide, 4 prairie species

The terns, like the gulls, are a group of seabirds that often range inland, far from the ocean. Terns are generally smaller than gulls and are more slender and graceful. Most have long, narrow, pointed wings and a forked tail. Many terns can hover in one spot and dive from the air to capture small fish and aquatic insects.

Terns fly in a light, buoyant manner, yet this relaxed flight can carry some of them, literally, to the ends of the Earth. The Arctic tern, for example, nests on the Arctic tundra in summer and winters in the pack ice of the Antarctic. To accomplish this, the bird makes an annual round-trip flight of up to 50,000 kilometers (30,000 mi.), the longest migration of any creature on the planet.

Field Identification
The Forster's tern has a deeply forked tail, black cap, orange legs, and an orange bill tipped with black. It is similar in size and color to the common tern, and even experienced birdwatchers mistake the two. Besides a slightly thicker bill, the Forster's tern tends to nest in widely scattered colonies in cattails and bulrushes, whereas the common tern frequently nests in dense colonies on islands.

Where to Find
This handsome tern is uncommon and is found in localized sloughs and marshes throughout the prairies.

Wintering Grounds
Forster's terns leave the prairies in August, and most of them winter in the coastal regions of the southern United States and Mexico. They return again by mid-May.

Diet and Feeding Habits
It is a delight to watch these accomplished aeronauts hover gracefully, dive, and swoop over the still waters of a prairie slough. In a dive, the bird may disappear underwater completely, only to surface almost immediately, clutching a silvery fish, a dragonfly nymph, or a water beetle in its colorful beak. In mid-flight, before they eat their catch, they usually shake themselves vigorously, producing a shower of water droplets that sparkle in the sun. The tern is equally adept at swooping over the water to pluck mayflies,

water striders, and dead insects from the surface, without even wetting a wingtip.

Breeding Biology

During courtship, the male Forster's tern feeds his mate. Such courtship feeding is common among terns. The behavior strengthens the bond between the pair and also improves the female's nutritional condition and prepares her for the energetic demands of egg laying. Female terns that are fed less often by their mates, produce lighter and fewer eggs. For a long time it was a mystery why underfed females did not simply feed themselves so that they could lay a full clutch of eggs. The probable reason is that a breeding female tern is too heavy to forage efficiently. An egg-heavy female weighs 50 percent more than she does at other times, and the added weight makes low-speed flight, hovering, and diving more difficult, so she relies on her mate for food.

Typically, Forster's terns nest in loose colonies in cattail sloughs and marshes. Usually they build a floating mat of vegetation, but sometimes they use an old muskrat house or steal a nest from a grebe. The usual clutch of three eggs is incubated by both partners for roughly three weeks. While one bird sits on the nest, the other scans the skies and defends their territory against trespassers. They aggressively dive-bomb Franklin's gulls and other terns. The chicks leave the nest a few days after hatching, as soon as they are able to swim, hide, and sneak through the cattails, but are fed by their parents until they begin to fly.

A female Forster's tern screams to her mate who is flying towards her with a silvery fish in his beak.

Black Tern
Chlidonias niger

Family Details
Tern Family, 44 species worldwide, 4 prairie species
See Forster's Tern for a general discussion of the Tern Family.

Field Identification
The distinctive black head and black belly plumage of this tern readily distinguish it from other prairie terns, which all have white undersides. The legendary American ornithologist Arthur Cleveland Bent

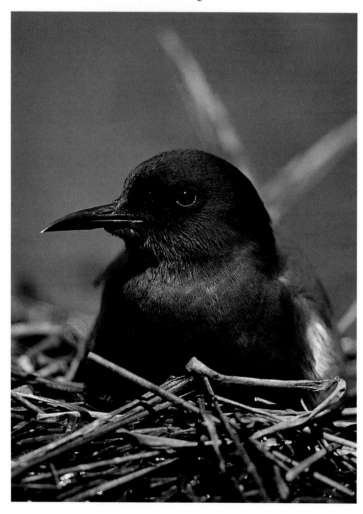

The black tern may occasionally build its nest on the top of an old muskrat house.

described the tern as "a restless waif of the air, flitting about hither and thither with a wayward, desultory flight, light and buoyant as a butterfly."

Where to Find
The black tern is found in wetlands throughout central North America, but is most abundant in the fertile sloughs and marshes of the northern prairies.

Wintering Grounds
Adult terns may migrate south as early as the end of July, and juveniles follow a month later. Most of these birds winter along the Pacific coast of Mexico and Central America and the northern coast of South America. In winter, the terns feed offshore, usually within 30 kilometers (18.5 mi.) of the coast. Flocks of a thousand birds or more may gather in good feeding areas. These delightful "marsh swallows" return to the prairies by mid-May.

Diet and Feeding Habits
The black tern forages low over the water, usually within 3 meters (10 ft.) of the surface. This acrobatic flyer skims spiders, beetles, and amphipods from the surface, and snatches mayflies and moths from the swaying heads of cattails and bulrushes. It will even chase and outmaneuver fast-flying dragonflies. Black terns, unlike many other terns, rarely plunge-dive, preferring to hawk for their food on the wing.

Breeding Biology
Black terns mate with a new partner every season. Bachelor males begin to advertise for a mate with "food flights." The hopefuls fly low over the slough carrying a shiny fish or large dragonfly, and call out loudly to make themselves more conspicuous. Interested females follow, and beg for the food. Once a pair has formed, the male continues to feed his new mate, and copulation is almost always preceded by a gift of food (a strangely familiar behavior!). In one study, a male black tern, at the height of mating, fed his partner 14 times in two hours and mated with her three times.

The black tern nests in small, loose colonies in shallow marshes and sloughs, and along the reed-covered margins of lakes. Colonies may contain up to 50 pairs, usually spaced from 5 to 20 meters (16–65 ft.) apart. The nests are small, flimsy piles of vegetation built in shallow water, and the eggs often become soaked. To combat this, black tern eggs have 50 percent more pores in their shells, an adaptation that keeps the inside of the eggs from becoming critically waterlogged.

Both sexes incubate the average clutch of three eggs, and they change places frequently, taking short shifts of just 30 to 60 minutes. When the chicks finally hatch after three weeks, both adults brood and feed the young. The hard-working parents may deliver 46 damselflies to the nest in a single hour. The youngsters grow swiftly and make their first flight at around three weeks of age. By this time the fledgling terns can feed themselves, but the parents may continue to supplement the young birds' diets for several weeks afterwards.

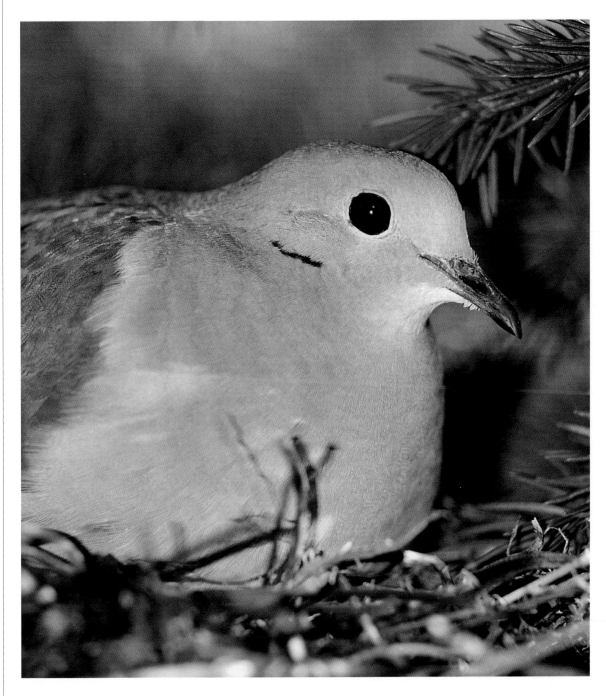

Mourning Dove

Zenaida macroura

Family Details

Pigeon and Dove Family,
309 species worldwide, 2 prairie species

Everyone who has seen a pigeon in a city park can recall the general appearance of the birds in this large family. Pigeons and doves vary greatly in size but all have a small head, a compact body, short legs, and a short beak. Some doves are no larger than a sparrow, and some pigeons, such as the crowned pigeon of New Guinea, are as large as a turkey.

Most pigeons and doves are strong flyers, and many have very large flight muscles, comprising up to 44 percent of their body weight, one of the highest proportions in any group of birds. Compare this with grebes, which are at the other extreme. These heavy-bodied, weak flyers have skimpy flight muscles that make up just 14 percent of their body weight.

One of the most intriguing aspects of the biology of pigeons and doves is their habit of feeding their young with "milk." This highly nutritious food, which resembles cottage cheese, has more than twice as much fat and seven times as much protein as cow's milk. Both parents produce the specialized "milk" in their crops (a pouch in the esophagus), and regurgitate the rich food to their newly hatched chicks.

Field Identification
The mourning dove is a streamlined, robin-sized bird that is grayish brown above and tan underneath. The dove takes flight with a characteristic whistling flutter, and when flying, the white edges of its long,

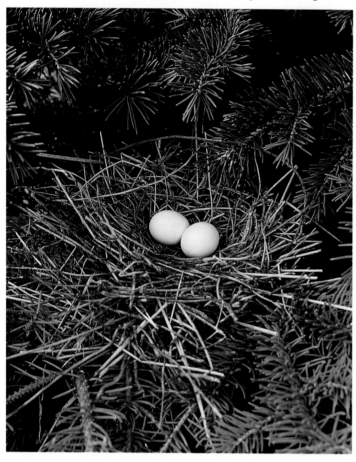

In the northern prairies, most pairs of mourning doves raise two or three clutches of eggs in a season.

tapered tail are clearly visible. At close range, you may notice the bluish skin around the bird's eyes, and its dull red feet and legs. The dove produces a soft, mournful croon that is the origin of its common name.

Where to Find
The mourning dove is widespread throughout the prairies. It is equally at home in native grasslands, farmlands, and urban parks, but avoids thick stands of trees.

Wintering Grounds
The doves of the northern Great Plains generally winter throughout the central and southern United States. In recent years, the popularity of bird feeders

has encouraged some of these hardy birds to winter on the prairies. Mourning doves can withstand extremely cold temperatures if they have an ample supply of food, but their toes can become frostbitten, and sometimes their fleshy feet freeze to the metal on bird feeders; such doves must be rescued.

Diet and Feeding Habits
The mourning dove's diet consists almost exclusively of the seeds of grasses, wildflowers, and farm crops. Typically, the dove feeds on the ground, quickly filling its crop, then flies to a roost away from predators, to slowly digest its meal. Seeds are swallowed whole and are ground up in the muscular gizzard, with the aid of grit and gravel, which the birds ingest for this purpose.

Breeding Biology
Flocks of mourning doves return to the prairies in late April or early May. Each hopeful male may coo from a dozen perches trying to lure a mate to his side. When an interested female lands near him, he coos even more loudly, dips and bows, and gently nibbles the feathers on her head and neck, trying to convince her that he is the dandiest dove of them all.

The mourning dove builds a flimsy nest of grass stems and twigs. In the prairies, I have found nests on the ground, but more often they are located in thick shrubbery. The caragana bushes and conifers planted as shelterbelts around farmhouses are a common nest site. Normally, the doves lay two bright white eggs, which the adults must cover continuously because they are so conspicuous. The male and female share the two-week incubation, and both parents feed the nestlings "crop milk" until the young are three or four days old. The young doves, called squabs, fledge after another two weeks, by which time they are fed nothing but seeds. The male parent continues to feed the squabs for another 12 days after they fledge, while the female prepares to lay a second clutch of eggs. In the southern United States, a female mourning dove may lay five or six clutches in a single nesting season; in the northern prairies, two is probably the maximum.

Trivia Tidbit
The most successful dove in the world is the rock dove, the familiar pigeon, which occurs in most cities and towns worldwide. This common dove has probably been studied more than any other bird and has helped scientists untangle the mysteries of flight, navigation, learning, inheritance, and numerous other aspects of avian biology.

Long-eared Owl

Asio otus

Family Details

Owl Family, 161 species worldwide, 10 prairie species

Owls, with their big eyes and large, swivelling heads, are recognizable to everyone. They are mainly nocturnal birds of prey, and have evolved an array of adaptations to hunt in darkness. The retina of an owl's eye, for example, is densely packed with sensitive light detectors that enable the bird to see well at night, although as a tradeoff, it probably has very weak color vision. The feathers on its face are shaped like a disk, which concentrates sounds and increases the sensitivity of the bird's hearing. As well, in many species, the external ear openings sit at slightly different heights on the sides of the bird's head. This helps the owl to more accurately pinpoint sounds and capture prey in complete darkness.

Owls, like most birds of prey, have a sharp, hooked beak and strong, talon-tipped feet. The birds generally swallow their prey whole, and regurgitate the indigestible parts of a meal as compact pellets several hours later.

In all species of owls the sexes look alike, and in nearly all of them their plumage is a cryptic mix of brown, gray, black, tan, and white. The body feathers of the birds are surprisingly soft, and the edges of their wing feathers have a comblike fringe. Both of these features help to muffle sound and make their flight as quiet as a heartbeat.

Field Identification

The long-eared owl may be confused with the larger great horned owl since both birds have a rusty-colored facial disk, bright yellow eyes, and long feathered ear tufts. The long-eared owl is a smaller, more secretive owl. Its ear tufts are closer together and more upright than those of the great horned owl, whose ear tufts point outward and are spaced farther apart.

Where to Find

The long-eared owl is found throughout the prairies, in wooded coulees and river valleys. This elusive raptor is strictly nocturnal and is seldom seen, although you might not believe it when you look at the photograph of the owl above perched on a fencepost in

The feathered ear tufts on the long-eared owl have nothing to do with hearing but are used for display.

broad daylight. This was an extremely unusual owl, and I have never found another like it. Most often these owls spend the day hidden in thick vegetation, especially conifers, where they perch close to the trunk and rely on the vertical streaking in their plumage to camouflage them.

Wintering Grounds

Although some long-eared owls may winter in the prairies, many of them, especially the more northern birds, migrate to the gentler climes farther south in the central and southern United States. Some migrate even farther. An owl banded in Saskatchewan was later recovered in Oaxaca, Mexico, 4000 kilometers (2485 mi.) away.

Diet and Feeding Habits

The long-eared owl likes to nest and roost in dense vegetation, although it forages in open habitats, such as fields and meadows. It has large wings for its size, and it hunts by systematically coursing back and forth close to the ground, sometimes hovering when it needs extra time to pinpoint a small rodent hidden in the grass. The owl has particularly sensitive hearing and relies as much, if not more, on hearing than it does on vision to locate and capture prey in darkness.

The long-eared owl is primarily a small-mammal specialist, preying on ground squirrels, voles, deer mice, pocket mice, kangaroo rats, pocket gophers, and at least four kinds of bats. Occasionally, the owl also hunts songbirds, lizards, and small snakes.

Breeding Biology

The breeding season for long-eared owls begins in March and April. The female owl does most of the incubation, and she is likely the one that selects the nest site. In an Idaho study, most of the owls chose to set up house in the old stick nests of black-billed magpies and crows. The new tenants generally make no renovations to the nest, although a few feathers may be added to the lining. The female owl sheds feathers from an area on her belly that becomes the bare brood patch used to heat her eggs. The feathers from her brood patch are used to line the nest.

A long-eared owl may lay as many as eight glossy white eggs, but a clutch of four or five is more common. Throughout the month-long incubation, the male feeds his mate. The female remains on the eggs almost constantly, except for an occasional short break or two at night, when darkness makes the eggs less vulnerable to detection by predators. The male continues to provision his entire family for two weeks after the chicks hatch, while the female broods the young. The young owlets can fly and hunt for themselves when they are two months old, and by this time both parents have deserted them.

Great Horned Owl

Bubo virginianus

Family Details

Owl Family, 161 species worldwide, 10 prairie species
See Long-eared Owl for a general discussion of the Owl Family.

Field Identification

The great horned owl is one of the most inspiring birds of prey on the prairies. Whether sitting on a nest or flying, it looks huge. It has a body weight of 1.8 kilograms (4 lb.) and a 1.6-meter (5.3 ft.) wingspan. Among owls, only the snowy is larger and more powerful. The great horned owl's bright yellow eyes and long ear tufts distinguish it from all other large owls, and its size and bulk alone separate it from the smaller and slimmer long-eared owl.

Where to Find

The horned hooter is the most widespread owl in the Americas, ranging from the Arctic treeline in North America to the wind-swept beech forests of Tierra del Fuego, at the southern tip of South America. This large, adaptable owl is a relatively common resident of the prairies, found in wooded coulees, badlands, farm shelterbelts, and urban woodlands. The owl is largely nocturnal, and during the day it hides motionless in a tree or thick shrubbery.

Wintering Grounds

The hardy great horned owl is a year-round citizen of the prairies. In *The Birds of Alberta*, authors Ray and Jim Salt wrote: "In winter, conifers are often chosen for daytime roosts since they provide shelter from the wind and snow, as well as from the eyes of magpies and jays that are always ready to mob a sleepy owl."

Diet and Feeding Habits

This large, powerful owl is a threat to a great variety of furred and feathered creatures on the prairies. It hunts cottontails, jackrabbits, ground squirrels, pocket gophers, voles, mice, red fox pups, muskrats, and sometimes house cats. Even the noxious spray of the striped skunk does not deter this taloned terror of the coulees. Remarkably, the great horned owl will attack and kill porcupines. Punishment was dealt to one owl that had 84 quills embedded in its face, sides, and legs.

The versatile great horned owl also hunts ducks,

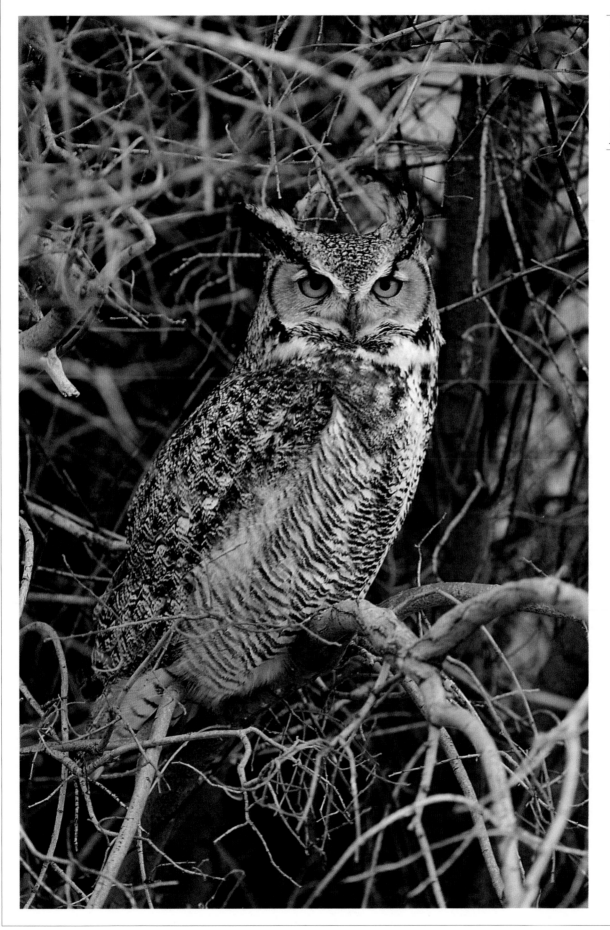

The plumage of prairie great horned owls is often paler than that of great horned owls that live in the forests.

Young great
horned owls are
dependent upon
their parents for
food until they
are about three
months old.

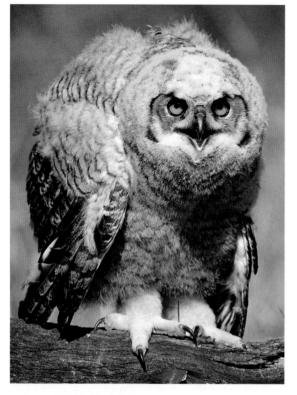

very dangerous, made even more so by the total unexpectedness with which they strike."

The great horned owl usually lays a clutch of two or three white eggs, which the female incubates alone for roughly 30 days, while her smaller mate hunts and feeds her. Young owlets begin to fly when they are seven weeks old, but take another three weeks to become proficient. Learning to hunt takes even longer, and the young fledglings may be fed by their parents well into the summer.

Short-eared Owl

Asio flammeus

Family Details
Owl Family, 161 species worldwide, 10 prairie species
See Long-eared Owl for a general discussion of the Owl Family.

Field Identification
The short-eared owl might better be called the no-eared owl since the small feathered tufts on its head are rarely visible. Watch for a pale, streaked owl with long, broad wings that hunts during the day. Its flight is mothlike and buoyant as it glides and flaps close to the ground. The owl flies very much like the northern harrier, but the two birds can be distinguished by the large, white rump patch on the harrier.

coots, pheasants, grouse, crows, blue jays, gulls, shore-birds, grebes, bitterns, and even great blue herons. In the Sonoran Desert of Baja, Mexico, I once flushed a great horned owl just after it had killed an adult peregrine falcon. On the northern prairies, the rapacious owls hunt these fast-flying falcons, as well as other raptors including long-eared owls, short-eared owls, burrowing owls, and red-tailed hawks.

Breeding Biology
The great horned owl is the earliest bird to nest on the prairies, sometimes laying eggs in the last week of February, when winter still firmly grips the land. Like many owls, the great horned rarely builds its own nest, preferring to use a natural cavity in a cliff face, or the abandoned nest of a crow or hawk. Occasionally the owls will even nest on the ground, and their aggressiveness insures that only the boldest, or most foolish, of predators would dare to approach such a nest. Several times I have been attacked by a great horned owl when I tried to photograph its nest in a tree, but I always wore a helmet and protective cloth-ing and was never injured. In *The Owls of North America*, author Allan Eckert described others who were not so fortunate: "There is no dearth of tales about the incredible savagery with which the great horned owl attacks a foe or defends itself, nor is there need for exaggeration of any kind. There are scores of well-authenticated cases on record where men have been blinded and suffered severe injuries to head, throat, chest, back, and groin by enraged attacking great horned owls. The attacks are bold, slashing, and

The fringed edge
on a short-eared
owl's wing
feathers muffles
sound and makes
the bird's flight
noiseless.

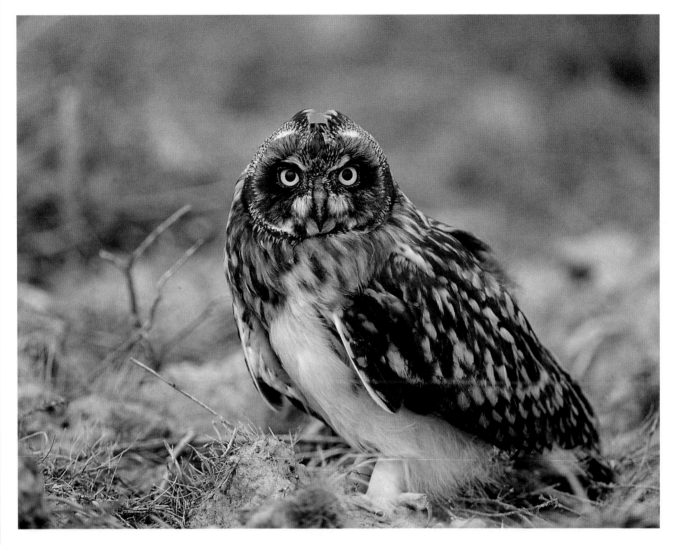

Where to Find
The short-eared is an open country owl that hunts and nests in grasslands, marshes, sloughs, and stubble fields. The bird is a gypsy, and moves around searching for concentrations of voles. Owl numbers vary drastically from year to year in direct relationship with the rise and fall of the local rodent population. During a vole plague, for example, several thousand owls may be present in an area, and the following year there may be none.

Wintering Grounds
Most short-eared owls from the Canadian prairies migrate into the United States. Frequently, these owls winter in loose groups of up to 200 birds. These owl gatherings may result because of a local abundance of prey, or because, as a group, they are better able to detect predators.

Diet and Feeding Habits
The life and times of the prairie short-eared owl are closely tied to vole numbers, which follow a three- to four-year cycle similar to that of Arctic lemmings.

When voles are abundant, the owls may hunt nothing else but these furry rodents. When voles are scarce, short-eareds will hunt moles, shrews, weasels, pocket gophers, and mice. They will also catch small numbers of songbirds and shorebirds. The short-eared owl, in common with most owls, is a visual and acoustic hunter, using both eyesight and hearing to locate its prey.

The short-eared owl has noticeably large wings for its size. In the jargon of aeronautical engineering, the owl has very low wing-loading, and this benefits the bird in several ways. It gives the owl better aerial agility and also a slow flight speed, which allows it more time to scan the ground. The low wing-loading also lessens the noise of its wings so that it can hear better in flight and is less likely to frighten its prey.

The short-eared owl frequently hunts and nests in the same habitats as those used by the northern harrier, and the two raptors often antagonize each other. There are many records of owls chasing harriers, and of harriers harassing owls and pirating their prey. In the end, the owl rules at night and the harrier during the day.

The short-eared owl commonly hunts during the day although it is equally adept at night.

Breeding Biology

The male short-eared owl frequently courts his mate during the day, so the details of his "sky dance" are well known. With the attentive female sitting on the ground, the displaying male quickly climbs in the sky through a series of small circles. Once he is about 60 to 90 meters up (200–300 ft.), he dives steeply, clapping his wings five to ten times beneath his body. Throughout the aerial performance, the male hoots continuously. At the bottom of the dive he swoops skyward and starts to circle and climb all over again. Short-eared owls pair with a different partner every breeding season, and it is important for a male to perform well to attract a partner.

The short-eared owl nests on the ground, usually on dry prairie or in a stubble field. Typically, the nest is a hollow scrape on the ground sparsely lined with grasses and downy feathers. When food is plentiful, the owls may nest in loose colonies. In a Montana study, the researchers found 30 nests in an area of just 164 hectares (405 acres). Two of the nests were just 55 meters (180 ft.) apart.

A well-fed short-eared owl may lay as many as 14 glossy white eggs. The hardworking male provisions his mate during the entire month-long incubation and then feeds the chicks as well until they are large enough to be left uncovered by the female. The young owlets leave the nest after two weeks, but do not fly until they are roughly one month old. The parents continue to feed the youngsters for several weeks after fledging.

Burrowing Owl

Athene cunicularia

Family Details

Owl Family, 161 species worldwide, 10 prairie species

See Long-eared Owl for a general discussion of the Owl Family.

Field Identification

The burrowing owl is a small owl, only 23 centimeters (9 in.) tall, with long legs, yellow eyes, and no ear tufts. The bird usually roosts on the ground, but sometimes perches on fenceposts.

Young burrowing owls hatch two to three days apart so a family of chicks always varies in age.

Where to Find

The owl is an uncommon resident of short-grass and mixed-grass prairies throughout the Great Plains. In recent years, habitat destruction and/or alteration, and poisoning by pesticides has caused owl numbers to decline at an alarming rate throughout most of their range. Formerly, the burrowing owl was closely associated with prairie dog towns, but black-tailed prairie dog populations have been reduced by 95 percent since 1900.

Wintering Grounds

Burrowing owls leave the northern Great Plains between early September and mid-October. Birds from the Canadian prairies, Montana, and North Dakota migrate as least as far south as Texas and northern Mexico. From the recovery of bands, it seems that Canadian burrowing owls may migrate farther south than owls in the United States, suggesting a "leap-frog" migration. These charming little owls return to the northern prairies in April.

Diet and Feeding Habits

The burrowing owl, like the short-eared owl, is another prairie owl that hunts in the daytime as well as at night. During the day, these insect exterminators prey on dung beetles, carrion beetles, crickets, and grasshoppers in the vicinity of their nest. Recently, I spent nine hours watching a mother owl resting on the mound, at the mouth of her nest burrow. Throughout that day, the vigilant mother repeatedly sprinted across the prairie on pencil-thin legs to slam a taloned foot on top of a large, juicy grasshopper that had made the fatal mistake of landing nearby.

At night their diet switches to rodents, with deer mice and voles as the most common prey. During their nocturnal hunts, the owls forage farther from the nest, up to 5 kilometers (3 mi.) away.

Breeding Biology

The burrowing owl, as its name suggests, nests underground. The male and female work together to renovate the abandoned burrow of a ground squirrel, prairie dog, or badger. The pair dig with their beaks and kick the dirt backwards with their feet.

Commonly, the nest burrow consists of a tunnel, 2 to 3 meters (6.5–10 ft.) long, with an enlarged chamber at the end. In Alberta and other areas, the owls have the unusual habit of lining the tunnel and nest chamber with dried, shredded cattle manure. A researcher in Oregon speculates that the manure masks the owls' odor and hides their presence from keen-nosed predators, such as badgers and foxes. The manure may also attract dung beetles and provide the owls, especially youngsters, with a handy source of food.

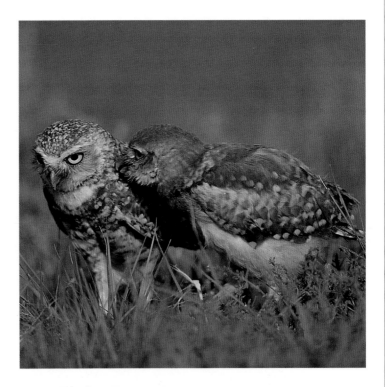

A pair of burrowing owls may raise 3 to 11 chicks. When chicks inside the burrow are frightened, they can mimic the buzzing sound of an angry rattlesnake. This interesting alarm vocalization may deter mammalian predators. The young owlets first emerge from the burrow when they are two weeks old, and in Alberta, this happens from the middle of May onwards.

As the youngsters grow, they cluster around the mouth of the burrow, waiting for the adults to feed them. While they are waiting, they hop about and flap their fluffy wings, preen each other, pick at debris on the ground, and chase beetles that crawl nearby. Young burrowing owls can fly by the time they are six weeks old.

Because burrowing owls are so small and nest on the ground, they are food for many predators. In Alberta the list includes badgers, coyotes, red foxes, striped skunks, least and long-tailed weasels, prairie rattlesnakes, and bullsnakes. Other predators attack from the sky, including Swainson's hawks, ferruginous hawks, northern harriers, prairie falcons, great horned owls, and short-eared owls. With that said, the burrowing owl is clearly the most hunted predator on the prairies.

Trivia Tidbits

Resident burrowing owls live throughout the grasslands of South America. Recently, I watched these owls in Brazil and couldn't determine what food the birds were hunting. I solved the mystery one night in the rain. The owls were eating earthworms.

A young burrowing owl chick preens the neck feathers of its parent.

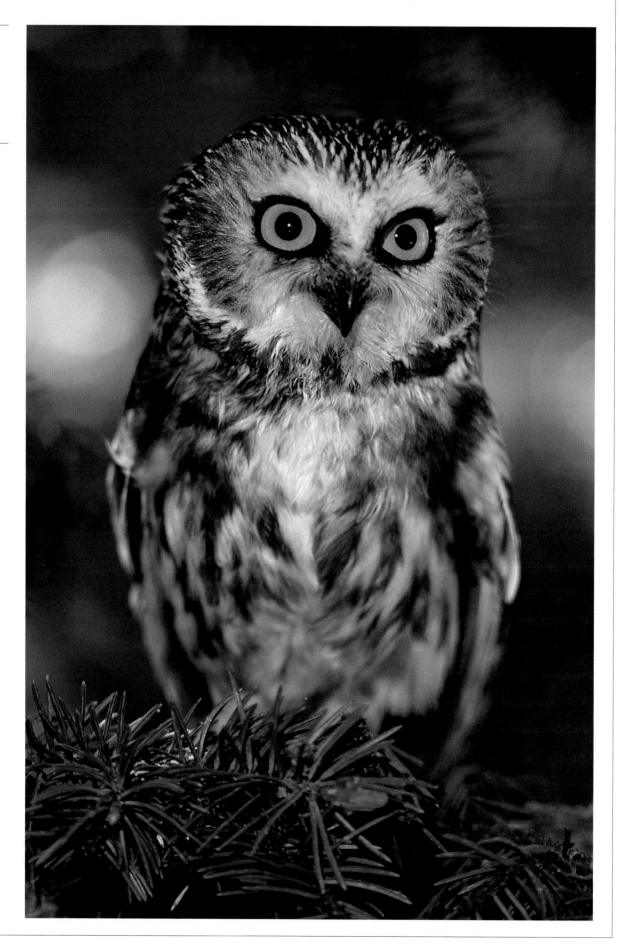

The forward-facing eyes of a northern saw-whet owl, as in all owls, give the bird better depth perception.

Northern Saw-whet Owl

Aegolius acadicus

Family Details

Owl Family, 161 species worldwide, 10 prairie species

See Long-eared Owl for a general discussion of the Owl Family.

Field Identification

The northern saw-whet is a mere 19 centimeters (7.5 in.) tall, and is the smallest owl in the prairies. The bird's size alone, and the absence of feathered ear tufts identify this attractive little owl.

Where to Find

The northern saw-whet lives mainly along wooded river valleys and in the aspen parklands that fringe the northern edge of the prairies. The saw-whet is strictly nocturnal, and hides in dense shrubbery during the day. The little owl is remarkably tame, so much so that researchers can sometimes catch the birds with their bare hands. The whistled notes of the males in spring may be the only indication that the owls are around.

Wintering Grounds

The winter behavior of saw-whets is not well understood, and it may vary from year to year. It may even vary among individuals from the same area. Three saw-whets banded near Edmonton, Alberta, illustrate this point. One of the owls wintered just 50 kilometers (30 mi.) southeast of where it was banded. Another was found 800 kilometers (500 mi.) away on the coast, in Vancouver, British Columbia, and the third wintered in North Dakota, 1000 kilometers (600 mi.) southeast of Edmonton.

Diet and Feeding Habits

The northern saw-whet is literally a night owl, and usually starts to hunt a half-hour after sunset and ends a half-hour before sunrise. Typically, the owl sits motionless on a low perch and waits for unwary prey to reveal itself. In this way, the patient predator catches small mammals, such as voles, mice, shrews, and chipmunks, as well as songbirds, including chickadees, kinglets, pine siskins, juncos, and sparrows.

The saw-whet is too small an owl to swallow its prey whole, so it must tear it into pieces, and often the prey is too large to be entirely eaten in a single meal. Surplus food is usually cached on a branch and retrieved later. In winter, if stored food freezes before it can be eaten, the resourceful owl thaws it out by sitting on it and warming it as it would an incubated egg.

Breeding Biology

The saw-whet owl nests, almost exclusively, in old woodpecker holes, and on the prairies, the nesting holes are usually those of northern flickers. The owls move indoors in April and lay five or six white eggs directly on the wood chips, on the floor of the nest cavity. The saw-whet male must be one of the hardest-working fathers in the Owl Family. The male feeds the female while she is laying her eggs, while she is incubating, and for three weeks after the chicks hatch. Not only this but he often feeds the chicks entirely by himself, bringing meals to them for a month after they have fledged and left the nest hole.

Snowy Owl

Nyctea scandiaca

Family Details

Owl Family, 161 species worldwide, 10 prairie species

See Long-eared Owl for a general discussion of the Owl Family.

Field Identification

The snowy owl is a large, white owl with penetrating golden yellow eyes. An adult female may weigh nearly 3 kilograms (6.6 lb.) and have a wingspan of 1.8 meters (5.9 ft.), making it the heaviest, most powerful owl in North America. The plumage of most adult males is almost pure white, whereas that of many adult females is barred and spotted with dark brown.

Where to Find

The snowy is a welcome winter visitor to the prairies. Telephone poles are a popular hunting perch for these owls, and an afternoon drive along a prairie highway in winter may yield half a dozen sightings or more.

Wintering Grounds

When food is available, many snowy owls, especially territorial males, remain in their Arctic breeding grounds for the winter, enduring blizzards, numbing cold, and weeks of continuous darkness. When the lemming population crashes, great numbers of these

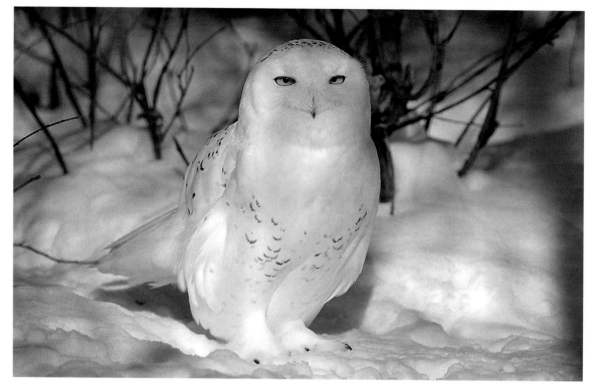

magnificent owls migrate into the northern Great Plains. In exceptional years, a few snowy owls may even fly as far south as Florida, Texas, and central California.

Diet and Feeding Habits

The "tundra ghost" of the Arctic has always fascinated me, and I have watched these birds numerous times on their northern breeding grounds. I wrote about them in *A is for Arctic: Natural Wonders of a Polar World*: "The snowy owl preys on lemmings, and indeed, the bird may eat three to five of the small furry rodents a day, consuming 600 to 1,600 of them in a single year. In a four-month summer nesting season, a pair of adult snowy owls and their brood of six to eight chicks may gulp down as many as 2,600 lemmings and still be hungry for more. Somehow, though, this heavyweight owl with its large, powerful feet and strong, sharpened talons, seems a little over-armed to tackle the lightweight lemming, which is a skimpy 70 grams (2.5 oz.)." The reason for the heavy-duty weaponry becomes clear when the owl migrates to the prairies in winter. There they may hunt jackrabbits and cottontails, grouse, pheasants, ducks, and geese. One winter, on the outskirts of Vancouver, the big owls specialized in house cats.

Breeding Biology

Snowy owls breed from the Arctic treeline north to the limit of land. One August, I photographed a pair of downy owl chicks on northern Ellesmere Island, just 150 kilometers (93 mi.) from the northern tip of

the continent. Male snowy owls set up breeding territories in April, and the females begin to lay eggs in May. The number of eggs she lays depends on the lemming population. In years when the rodents are scarce, the females may lay no eggs at all, but in boom years she may have a clutch of 11—the largest clutch of any bird in the Arctic. The young owlets leave the nest when they are 25 days old and continue to be fed entirely by their parents for at least another five weeks, when they finally begin to hunt for themselves. Even then, the inexperienced young owls are partially fed for several more weeks.

Trivia Tidbit

All owls regurgitate compact pellets of indigestible hair, feathers, bones, teeth, claws, and insect parts, 3 to 12 hours after they have eaten. A large owl, such as the great horned owl, may spit up a pellet 13 centimeters (5 in.) long and shaped like a stubby cigar, whereas the pellets from a burrowing owl are usually pencil-thin and just 3 centimeters (1.2 in.) long. An owl will often regurgitate pellets where it regularly roosts, and they may accumulate on the ground. In prairie Alberta, my wife, Aubrey, collected more than 50 great horned owl pellets beneath a single roost tree. The dissection of pellets is the principal way biologists study an owl's diet.

Owl pellet analysis is also one of the best ways for researchers to survey small mammals. Because owls hunt such a broad range of prey, they are better at sampling the different rodents that live in an area than a biologist is with live traps.

Common Nighthawk

Chordeiles minor

Family Details

Nightjar Family, 83 species worldwide,
2 prairie species.

The unusual common name for members of this family is derived from their tendency to be active mainly after dark, and to produce loud calls that "jar" the silence of the night. Another common name for the family is goatsuckers, an equally intriguing moniker. This name comes from an ancient superstition dating from the time of Aristotle. All of the nightjars have a tiny beak but a very wide gape, and peasant farmers believed the birds clamped their large mouths to the udders of their livestock and milked them dry. In fact, nightjars are strictly insect eaters, and they net their prey on the wing using their large mouths. Since these birds sometimes swoop near grazing livestock to catch flying insects flushed by the animals, they were blamed for the poor milk production of the undernourished, pest-ridden farm animals. The stomach of an average nightjar is the size of a thimble and it would take quite a flock of these birds to milk a goat dry, not to mention the trouble they would have convincing an irascible old nanny to stand still while all this was happening.

Field Identification

The nighthawk is most often seen in flight. The grayish brown, robin-sized bird has long, pointed wings, each with a wide band of white in the center of the underwing. No other bird on the prairies has these conspicuous white wing bars. If you are lucky enough to find a nighthawk perched on a fencepost or on a branch in daylight, notice its large eyes and tiny beak.

Where to Find

A nighthawk might be found in any habitat in the prairies, or even in the center of a city. Formerly, these birds were common in urban centers because they would nest on flat gravel roofs and hawk for

The large eyes of the nocturnal nighthawk weigh more than the bird's brain.

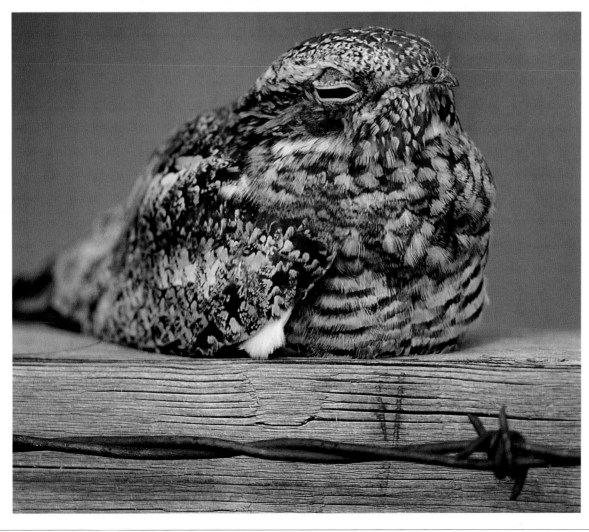

insects between the towering buildings. In recent years, these harmless birds have disappeared from many cities. Pesticide spraying for mosquitoes, and the popularity of rubberized rooftops that become hotter than gravel, are the main reasons for the decline.

Wintering Grounds
Prairie nighthawks winter in distant South America, mainly in Paraguay, Uruguay, and northern Argentina—a roundtrip of 16,000 kilometers (9940 mi.).

Diet and Feeding Habits
The common nighthawk has a simple diet containing all the major food groups: insects, insects, and more insects. Flying ants are the most common food, but the bird also scoops up beetles, bugs, and flies. One investigator examined a nighthawk that had eaten 2175 flying ants. Another bird had 500 mosquitoes in its stomach.

At one time, scientists believed that the nighthawk used echolocation to pinpoint insects in flight, but it now appears that it relies entirely on its sensitive vision. The eyes of all birds are relatively large, but those of the nighthawk are exceptionally so. In fact, the nighthawk's eyes weigh more than its brain.

Breeding Biology
The common nighthawk is silent most of the year except during the breeding season in June and early July when males court and "boom." Typically, an interested female sits on the ground like a spectator at an air show while her suitor performs in the sky above her. A nighthawk's boom sounds like someone blowing across the top of an empty bottle, and the sound is produced at the bottom of a power dive as air rushes through the stiff feathers at the tip of the male's wings. An enthusiastic boomer may dive 40 times in half an hour.

The nighthawk lays her two patterned eggs directly on the bare ground. The female incubates the eggs alone, and leaves them unattended at night, to feed. During the day, she covers the eggs continuously to protect them from the excessive heat of the sun. In the badlands of Alberta, for example, the ground temperature may exceed 50°C (122°F), and would quickly cook an exposed nighthawk egg. An incubating female cools herself, and her eggs, by evaporating moisture from the lining of her cavernous mouth, which is richly supplied with blood vessels for this purpose.

Nighthawk chicks are covered with down and can scuttle about soon after hatching. The male does most of the feeding of the twins, while the female broods them. The precocious young can fly before they are three weeks old.

Belted Kingfisher
Ceryle alcyon

Family Details
Kingfisher Family, 94 species worldwide,
1 prairie species

This is a family of small- to medium-sized birds that hover and dive for fish, snatch insects on the wing, and scoop lizards, snakes, and scorpions off the ground. They have stocky bodies, short necks, large heads, and long, thick, pointed bills. Many are brightly colored, in cinnamon and vibrant azure blue.

All of these handsome birds nest in holes of one kind or another, either in a riverbank, a tree, or a termite mound, and most of them lay glossy white eggs. In the darkened interior of a nest cavity, white eggs can be found more easily by the parents, and there is no need to camouflage them from predators since they are hidden inside a cavity.

Most kingfishers are noisy, and produce loud, shrill shrieks or chattering rattles. The boisterous call of Australia's laughing kookaburra is famous and has been used in countless Hollywood movies to depict the tropics. The kookaburra is one of the world's largest kingfishers.

Field Identification
The belted kingfisher is a medium-sized bird with a large, ragged crest. The bird is bluish gray on top and white underneath and has a broad, white collar. Both sexes have a bluish gray band across their chests, and the female has a rusty band across her belly as well. Generally, the kingfisher flies off in alarm and rattles loudly at the slightest disturbance, so you will probably hear the bird before you see it.

Where to Find
The noisy kingfisher may be found on any stream, river, pond, or lake in the prairies. The bird avoids muddy waters and those that are overgrown with vegetation, both of which make diving for fish more difficult.

Wintering Grounds
If there is open water for fishing, the bird can survive the cold of a prairie winter. Even so, most kingfishers migrate south, in October, to the coastal and inland waters of Mexico and Central America. The bird's familiar scolding rattle returns to the prairies in April.

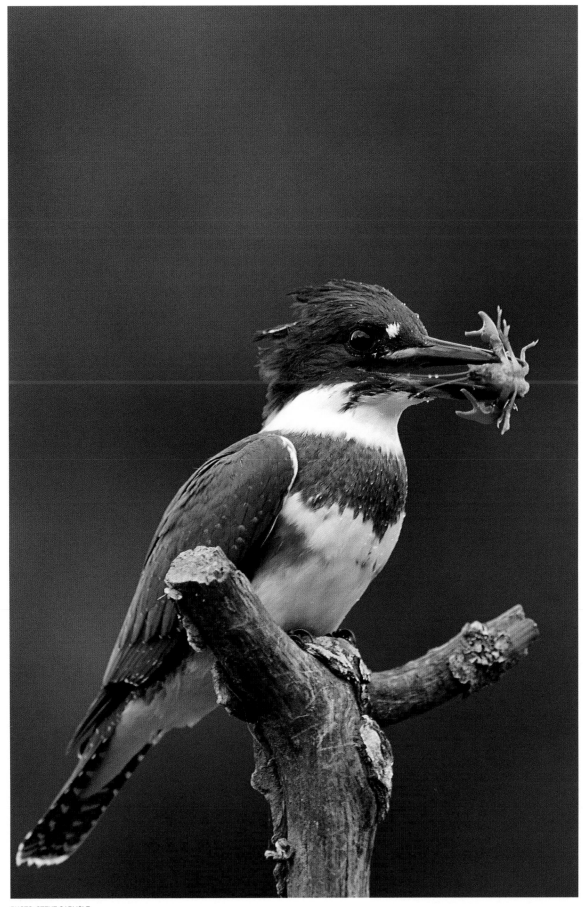

This male belted kingfisher may tenderize the crayfish by pounding it against the bird's perch.

Diet and Feeding Habits

Although the kingfisher is primarily a piscivore, or fish-eater, it also catches frogs, snakes, lizards, snails, and crayfish. Typically, the big-beaked bird hunts from a perch, usually a tree snag, a branch, or a telephone wire overhanging the water. It may also course along the shore, hover, and scan. Most of its fishing is done near the surface, and usually the kingfisher does not completely submerge in a dive. At the moment of impact, the bird closes its eyes and grabs the fish with its pincerlike beak. It carries the wiggling prey to a branch, where it repeatedly pounds it against the wood. This compulsory "tenderizing" breaks the spines off catfish and sticklebacks, and stuns the prey so that it can be swallowed head first in a single gulp. Kingfishers, in common with birds of prey, disgorge compact pellets of undigested bones and fish scales after they have eaten. Biologists dissect these pellets to learn which fish the birds are eating.

Breeding Biology

The kingfisher nests in a hole, usually in a bank along a shoreline, but occasionally in a gravel pit or a road cut far from water. Both adults peck and shovel, for up to a week, to dig a tunnel 1 to 2 meters (3–6 ft.) deep, with a small, round chamber at the end. On shorelines, the tunnel entrance is dug high enough above the water to avoid flooding, yet far enough below the top of the bank to keep predators from sneaking inside.

The birds lay five to seven glossy white eggs, which both parents incubate for the 22 days it takes for the pink, naked nestlings to hatch. Researcher Dr. Michael Hamas jokingly remarked that the homely youngsters "chatter continuously and huddle together, forming a cluster of interlocking heads and wings."

Young kingfisher chicks do not produce feces packaged in a convenient mucous sac that can be carried away by the parents, as is common in most songbirds. Instead, they point their butts at the wall and squirt away. Afterwards, they spin around and peck the earth above where they blasted. This loosens the soil, which buries the feces and keeps the nest chamber clean. The fledglings leave the nest burrow at a month old, and are fed by both parents for three weeks afterwards.

Trivia Tidbit

The surest way for a belted kingfisher to escape the strafing talons of a peregrine falcon is to dive underwater.

Northern Flicker
Colaptes auratus

Family Details

Woodpecker Family, 215 species
worldwide, 5 prairie species

Woodpeckers are the original head-bangers. Their unique arboreal lifestyle has produced a number of special adaptations. They have a reinforced skull to protect their brain when they are drilling for food with their strong, chisel-like bills. Many woodpeckers have a long tongue that extends far beyond the tip of their bills. The tongue is coated with sticky saliva and tipped with barbs to extract woodboring grubs from crevices and ants from nests. The birds also have stiff, pointed tail feathers to prop themselves up, and strong leg muscles to stay anchored when they start to hammer.

Most of these hard-headed carpenters nest in holes that they excavate in the trunks of trees. Afterwards, their abandoned holes are used for shelter and as nest sites by a wide variety of birds, mammals, frogs, and snakes. Because old woodpecker holes are crucial to so many other animals the birds are often designated as a "keystone" species.

Woodpeckers are the only birds to drum rhythmically with their beaks to proclaim their territories and to advertise for mates. Normally, both sexes hammer on hollow, resonant branches and snags. Some of these hammerheads have discovered the marvel of metal, and they drum on eavestroughs, drainpipes, and trash cans, testing the patience of the most understanding homeowner.

Field Identification

The flicker is a medium-sized brown woodpecker with black barring on its back, a black bib, and black spots on its belly. Both sexes have a red patch on the nape of their neck, but only the male has a black "moustache." In flight, the woodpecker has a large, conspicuous white rump patch, and beautiful yellow underwings.

Where to Find

The northern flicker is a common, noisy resident of open woodlands and suburban areas throughout the prairies.

Wintering Grounds

Flickers from the northern prairies migrate into the southeastern United States in October, and return to their breeding grounds in late March and early April.

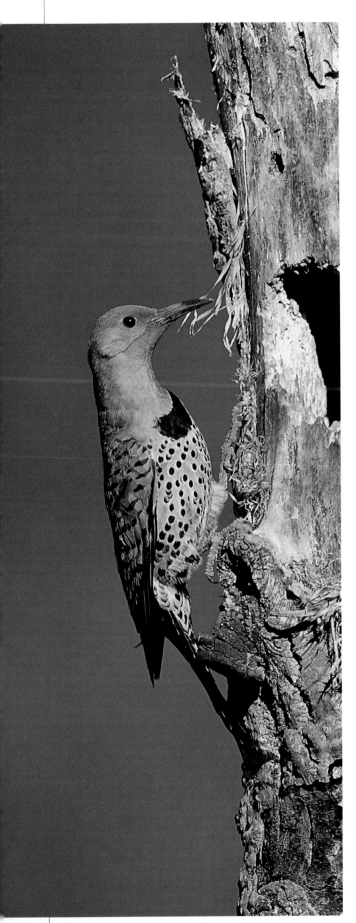

Diet and Feeding Habits

In winter, the flicker may forage on tree trunks in the usual woodpecker fashion, but most of the time it hunts on the ground, hopping about, hammering, and probing anthills with its powerful beak. The northern flicker eats more ants than does any other bird in North America. Of interest to those readers who love avian trivia, as I do, the name for a creature whose principal diet is ants is a myrmecophage. Now that's a challenging word to casually slip into a conversation.

Although they are ant specialists, flickers also eat ground beetles, crickets, wood lice, grasshoppers, butterflies, grubs, bugs, and caterpillars. In autumn, when most ants have moved underground, the bird's diet shifts to wild fruits, including those of sumac, dogwood, and poison ivy.

Breeding Biology

Researcher Dr. Lawrence Kilham compared the sound of a flicker drumming to a miniature pneumatic drill. During the breeding season, the paired birds each drum at established posts throughout their territory. The drum rolls, with roughly 25 beats, last a second, although you would need a sonograph to recognize this. Even so, the birds can tell the difference, and each species of woodpecker likely has a unique drumming pattern.

Flickers usually dig a nest cavity in a dead or diseased tree. Often the chosen trees are infected with heartrot fungus, which softens the inside of the tree, and makes it easier to excavate. The nest cavities are usually 5 to 8 meters (16–26 ft.) off the ground, but I have found some less than a meter (3 ft.) high.

The northern flicker lays an average of six white eggs. In these birds, and many others, the "feel" of the eggs against the female's belly seems to influence the size of her clutch, and she may continue to lay eggs until it feels right. One mother flicker produced 71 eggs in 73 days when an inquisitive researcher removed the eggs as quickly as they were laid.

Chick rearing is a family affair. Both parents incubate the eggs, brood and feed the chicks, and carry away the numerous fecal sacs produced by the nestlings. Young flickers fledge and leave the nest when they are around four weeks old.

Trivia Tidbit

The flicker occurs in three color variations. In the prairies, the bird is the "yellow-shafted" variety because of the color of its underwings. In the American Southwest the "gilded" flicker has yellow underwings, but has replaced its black moustache with a red one. West of the Rockies, the flickers have red underwings and are referred to as "red-shafted."

The stiff tail feathers of the flicker act as a strut to support the bird.

Yellow-bellied Sapsucker

Sphyrapicus varius

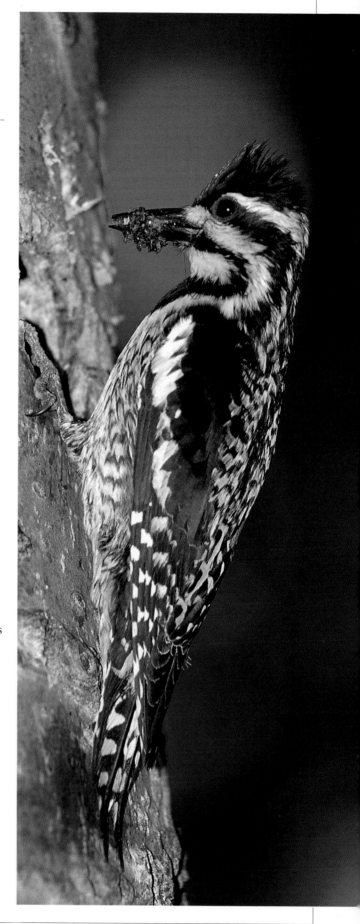

Family Details

Woodpecker Family, 215 species worldwide, 5 prairie species

See Northern Flicker for a general discussion of the Woodpecker Family.

Field Identification

The yellow-bellied sapsucker is a small, black-and-white woodpecker with a red forehead and crown, and a black bib. The male also has a red throat. The yellowish coloration on the bird's belly is often faint and difficult to see.

Where to Find

The sapsucker is found in woodlands throughout the prairies.

Wintering Grounds

Most sapsuckers take their sap-sucking south by late summer. The birds winter in the southern United States and Mexico, where the livin' is easy and the sap's still a-runnin'. The birds return to the prairies by the end of April.

Diet and Feeding Habits

The sapsucker is unusual among woodpeckers in having a sweet tooth. The bird drills horizontal rows of shallow pits in the bark of a tree. A single tree may contain more than 900 drill holes. The woodpecker waits for sap to well up in the holes and laps up the sugary fluid with the fringed tip of its tongue. Perhaps since the yellow-bellied sapsucker often has very little yellow on its belly, and the bird never sucks sap, but laps it up, I think it might be more logical to call the woodpecker the non-yellow-bellied sap-lapper.

Although the sapsucker prefers to drill and drink from aspens, poplars, and birches, its drill holes have been seen in at least 250 species of deciduous and coniferous trees. Many species profit from the labors of this little woodpecker. Hummingbirds, warblers, kinglets, and flying squirrels regularly visit the oozing wells for a sugar fix. The sweet sap also attracts flies and other insects, which the bird immediately adds to its diet. During the nesting season, sapsucker parents hunt spiders, tent caterpillars, hornets, wasps, ants, mayflies, and beetles to feed to their young. The growing nestlings require essential proteins and fats that tree sap does not contain.

A female sapsucker returns to its nest with a beak full of carpenter ants to feed its young.

Breeding Biology

Both sexes dig the nest hole, in the trunk of an aspen or poplar, although the male does three-quarters of the digging. The pair may begin at the end of April, and work for two to four weeks. The finished nest is a gourd-shaped cavity, commonly about 36 centimeters deep (14 in.). A tree cavity nest not only hides nestlings from the peering eyes of predators, but also protects the adults and young from chilling winds and driving rain, and buffers them against extremes of temperature.

Both parents incubate the half-dozen eggs, the female during the day and the male at night. The young, wrinkled sap-sippers hatch after two weeks, and both adults feed them. At one nest I watched the parents bring billfuls of carpenter ants almost every 10 minutes for the entire afternoon. When the chicks become large, the parents may make up to 24 feeding trips an hour. By the time the young woodpeckers are three weeks old, they are climbing to the nest opening and jostling with each other to stick their heads into the outside world. The young leave the nest seven to ten days later, and are fed by their haggard parents for another week afterwards.

Horned Lark
Eremophila alpestris

Family Details

Lark Family, 91 species worldwide, 1 prairie species

The larks are small songbirds that live in open grassy plains, deserts, and fields. These birds do most of their living on the ground. They hide on the ground, using their brown, streaky plumage to blend with the grass. They walk and feed on the ground, picking up insects and seeds. They court and mate on the ground, with chittering, fluttering, and waving of tails, and they nest on the ground, in hidden cups of grass, fur, and feathers. When a lark sings it finally leaves the ground, transforming itself from ordinary to outstanding. Most larks live where there are no trees on which to perch, so they sing on the wing, often high in the sky, and pour out their passion with elaborate, wild music.

In most groups of birds, the voice box, called the syrinx, is controlled by a single pair of muscles. In

The horned lark is one of the earliest songbirds to nest on the prairies, often beginning in April.

101

larks, and other songbirds, five to eight pairs of muscles control the syrinx and produce songs that are complex and beautiful. Each side of the syrinx, in fact, works independently, so a songbird can literally sing a duet with itself.

Field Identification

The horned lark is a small, brown bird with a white belly, black bib and eyeline, and small, feathered ear tufts that can be raised or lowered. In flight, the bird has a dark tail with white outer feathers. Females are duller in color than males, and have less prominent ear tufts.

Where to Find

The horned lark lives in Eurasia as well as in North America. It loves open country and big skies, and avoids forests. In the prairies, the lark is found in short and mixed grasslands, meadows, and bare fields.

Wintering Grounds

The horned lark is a year-round resident throughout most of its range in North America. However, birds in the extreme northern prairies of Canada migrate short distances south. They frequently mix with migratory snow buntings and longspurs, and may wander widely in large, nomadic flocks of several hundred birds. Horned larks are one of the first migrants to return to the prairies in spring, often arriving in February.

Diet and Feeding Habits

For most of the year, the horned lark is a seed eater that feeds on the ground. It likes bare soil and short grasses where it can find its food more easily, and where it has a clear view of the surroundings to watch for predators. In winter, it is frequently seen feeding in the fields, and flying from one snowfree patch to the next. During the breeding season, when the adults are feeding young, the larks' diet switches to beetles, grasshoppers, and caterpillars.

Breeding Biology

In 1927, ornithologist George Sutton described the voice of the horned lark as "a sweet and delicate tinkling." The horned lark is an early riser, and male songsters usually serenade the morning earlier than other prairie birds. Commonly they begin more than an hour and a half before sunrise and end their recital soon after the sun comes up. They start to sing again several hours before sunset. When a lark sings from the ground, the macho male likes to be elevated, even if that only means standing on the summit of a dried cow patty.

Males also sing on the wing. First, they rapidly and quietly climb up to a height of 100 to 250 meters (325–820 ft.); then, with their wings and tail spread, they glide and sing. In early spring, when the prairie seems desolate, the delicate music of the lark never fails to brighten my spirits. Such song flights may last up to eight minutes.

The horned lark lays two to five eggs in a hollow cup of feathers and grass on the ground. The female alone incubates the eggs, and the newly hatched nestlings are all mouths and appetites. The insides of their mouths are a vibrant yellow-orange marked with five black spots. The color and spot pattern stimulate the parents to bring food to their chicks and also serve as a "feeding target." In some songbirds, the spot pattern is different for closely related species, and parents will only feed chicks with the spot pattern for their own species.

Young horned larks leave the nest when they are about 10 days old and scatter nearby. Separated like this, the chicks are less vulnerable to predators. By four weeks of age, the young larks can fly well and feed themselves.

Barn Swallow

Hirundo rustica

Family Details

Swallow and Martin Family, 89 species worldwide, 7 prairie species

These popular and well-known small birds are skilled and graceful fliers. Their long, pointed wings give them speed and agility to catch insects in flight. Author John Terres wrote: "… in darting flight, [swallows] hold their tiny but wide-gaping mouths fully open to scoop hundreds of flying insects out of the air." Swallows have small feet and very short legs, and they dislike landing in the thick foliage of trees, so you will often see them perched on wire fences and telephone lines.

Some swallows thrive well around humans, and in North America, some species commonly nest on buildings and bridges. When I lived in California in the early 1980s, my wife and I went to the famous mission at San Juan Capistrano to witness the annual return of the cliff swallows. Apparently, the swallows first nested on the mission in 1776, and the legend claims that the punctual swallows returned every year after that on 19 March. Aubrey and I were on time, but the swallows were not, and we left before the birds finally arrived. Naturally, the cliff swallows of Capistrano are subject to weather delays, as they are everywhere else in the world.

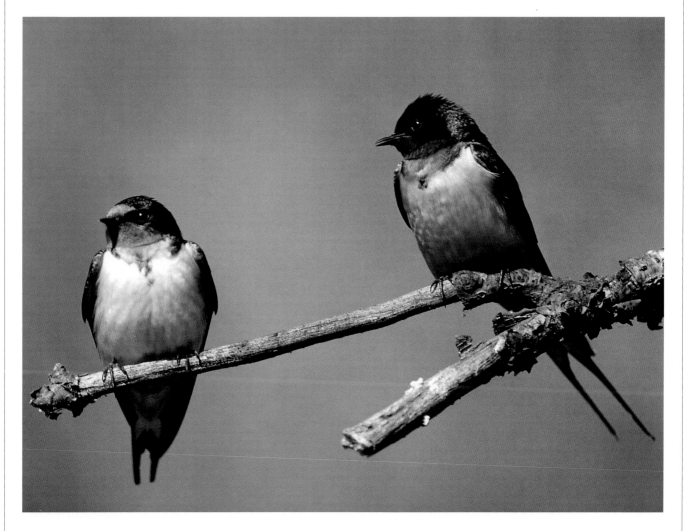

Field Identification
The long, deeply forked tail of the barn swallow is the best way to identify this handsome bird. The swallow is iridescent blue on top and bright cinnamon underneath, and has a rusty forehead and throat, making it the most colorful of the prairie swallows.

Where to Find
The barn swallow is common throughout the prairies, frequently nesting around buildings in rural and suburban areas.

Wintering Grounds
The barn swallow winters throughout the length of South America. It migrates via Mexico and Central America, travelling during the day in flocks that forage along the way. The swallow returns to the prairies by early May.

Diet and Feeding Habits
The agile barn swallow catches flying insects with the aerial agility common to all swallows. It hunts over fields, meadows, sloughs, and marshes. I've seen these delightful swallows follow a farmer cutting hay to catch insects frightened into flight by the machinery. The barn swallow also bathes and drinks on the wing, skimming the surface of the water.

Breeding Biology
Truthful advertising has always been the best way for a male bird to broadcast his attributes to potential mates. In the barn swallow, the male's long, forked tail is his most important ornament. In these birds, males infested with blood-sucking mites weigh less, have shorter tails, and produce fewer young than do healthy males. Females can detect the differences in tail length and use this information to select a mate. Infected male swallows also seem to recognize the superior quality and parenting ability of their longer-tailed male rivals. As a result, they sneak copulations with the female partners of these birds more often than they do with females paired with less healthy mates. Even though this behavior is instinctual, the logic in the strategy is clear. If you are a male, infested with parasites and unable to attract a mate, you can still perpetuate your genes by having a healthy male unknowingly raise your offspring.

Barn swallows nest in small colonies that may

A richly colored male barn swallow (right) courts a prospective mate.

contain several dozen pairs. Both partners build the cup-shaped nest using mud, grass stems, hair, and feathers, and cement it to the top of a beam or ledge, or plaster it against a vertical wall. The birds lay four or five glossy white eggs speckled with chocolate brown spots. Both parents incubate the eggs and feed the hungry hatchlings. The young swallows can fly by the time they are three weeks old, but for several days afterwards they may return at night to the familiar security of the nest to roost. The parents continue to feed the young on the wing for a week or so after they fledge.

Tree Swallow
Tachycineta bicolor

Family Details
Swallow and Martin Family, 89 species worldwide, 7 prairie species

See Barn Swallow for a general discussion of the Swallow and Martin Family.

The tree swallow nests in cavities, and both sexes share in gathering dry grass and feathers to line the nest.

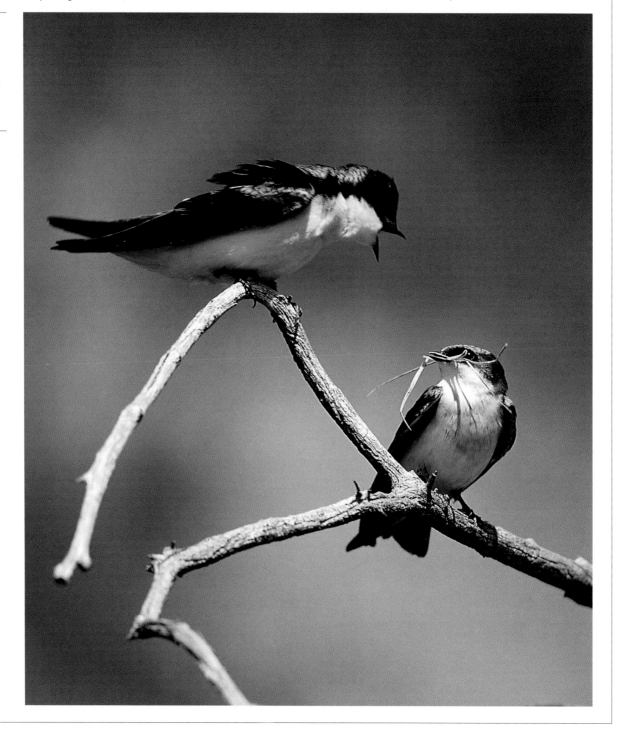

Field Identification

The tree swallow is a small, acrobatic bird with long, pointed wings and a notched tail. The bird is an iridescent greenish blue above, and white underneath.

Where to Find

This swallow is relatively easy to find in the prairies. Look near fields, native grasslands, and the margins of sloughs, marshes, and lakes. Conservation groups in many areas have erected nest boxes along fence lines for thousands of kilometers. As a result, tree swallows are more common in the prairies than they would normally be.

Wintering Grounds

Tree swallows leave the prairies in August, and migrate to the Gulf Coast of the southeastern United States, Mexico, and Central America. They return in April, much earlier than other prairie swallows. Their unique ability to digest seeds and fruits allows them to return early when cool weather may still keep their usual insect prey grounded and hard to find.

Diet and Feeding Habits

The tree swallow hunts insects on the wing using steep climbs, dives, and abrupt turns. It commonly forages over fields, cattail marshes, and open water. The agile swallow can swoop down and pluck prey from the surface of the water, and it does this to catch mayflies, caddisflies, and stoneflies. The birds also drink on the wing, gliding over the surface and slicing the water briefly with their open beak.

Breeding Biology

The swallow nests in an old woodpecker hole or natural cavity in a tree. The competition for such nest sites and the shortage of them have influenced the swallows' breeding behavior more than any other factor. The birds' early arrival in spring lets them claim a nest site as soon as possible, and once they do, they defend it with aggression. The pretty little tree swallow becomes a fierce tiger in the sky, and both sexes will fight to defend their home. Rival swallows will viciously peck each other's head and body in aerial combat, in skirmishes on the ground, in the confinement of a nest cavity, and even in the water. Losers may pay with their lives. The competition for nest sites doesn't end there. A homeless female swallow may enter an occupied nest and kill the nestlings, speeding up the desertion of the nest by the resident pair.

Tree swallows also fight with other species for nest cavities. House sparrows will kill adult swallows inside a cavity and then build their own nest on top of the carcass. House-hunting wrens will sneak into a swallow nest and puncture the eggs or peck the nestlings to death. The swallows, in turn, may kill both eastern and mountain bluebirds if they corner them in a cavity. When nest sites are scarce, the stakes are high, and the drive to reproduce forces many birds to battle with their lives.

Tree swallows usually raise four to six chicks. Both parents forage for the young, and a pair of adults may make 20 feeding trips an hour. The fledglings leave the nest cavity in late May and early June when they are only 18 to 22 days old. The parents feed them for another week or so after that while the young swallows hone their flying and hunting skills.

The popularity of bird houses has made the tree swallow a common sight along many prairie roadways.

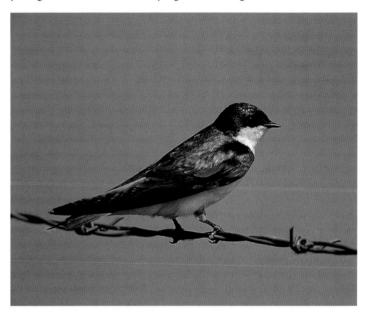

Cliff Swallow
Hirundo pyrrhonota

Family Details

Swallow and Martin Family,
89 species worldwide, 7 prairie species

See Barn Swallow for a general discussion of the Swallow and Martin Family.

Field Identification

The cliff swallow has a dark back, a white breast and belly, and a black throat. In flight, you can tell it apart from other prairie swallows by its square tail and reddish rump.

Where to Find

The cliff swallow originally nested exclusively on cliff faces in the western mountains. Beginning in the mid-1800s, the swallow gradually expanded its range eastward across the Great Plains into the eastern third of the continent, using buildings, bridges, and highway culverts as new nest sites. The adaptable swallow is now relatively widespread throughout the prairies.

Wintering Grounds
Cliff swallows leave the prairies soon after their chicks fledge. The migration begins in late July, and most are gone by the middle of August. They winter in the marshes and grasslands of Brazil, Paraguay, and Argentina. More than 50,000 swallows roosted in one wetland in northern Argentina. The swallows return to their prairie breeding grounds early in May.

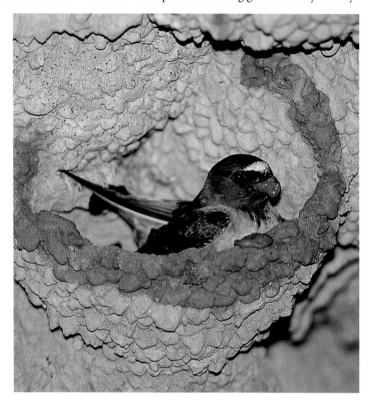

A pair of cliff swallows may take two weeks to build a nest and use 1000 pellets of mud.

Diet and Feeding Habits
The cliff swallow feeds mainly on flying insects. The birds often forage in groups, sometimes numbering several hundred individuals. The gregarious swallows target the mating swarms of different flies and midges, and also take insects that are carried aloft in thermals. Because these swarms of prey are patchy, an individual swallow benefits by hunting in a group and watching the success of its companions. Cliff swallows are the most social swallow in the world, and their large nesting colonies function as "informa-

tion centers." A hungry swallow can watch its neighbors when they bring food to their chicks, and follow one of them when it leaves on its next feeding trip. Information sharing, of course, is unintentional but benefits every individual in the colony. In the end, swallows that nest in large colonies forage more efficiently and deliver more food to their chicks than do those in small colonies.

Breeding Biology
The cliff swallow builds a gourd-shaped nest of mud about the size of a cantaloupe and attaches it to the vertical face of a cliff, building, or bridge. Several thousand pairs may nest together in a single large colony. When the first swallows return in the spring, they may claim an existing nest from the previous season. The most desirable nests are those that are not infested by blood-sucking parasites and those located in the center of the colony. Mud nests on the edge of a colony are more vulnerable to predators, especially bullsnakes that prey on eggs and nestlings, and occasionally ambush an adult. In a three-day period, during a study in Nebraska, one bullsnake pillaged dozens of nests and ate 150 eggs.

Cliff swallows fight for the best nests, pecking and tearing at each other with their beaks and beating each other with their wings. When all the old nests are taken, a pair will build a new one. The average mud nest consists of between 900 and 1200 mud pellets, and it takes the owners a week or two to construct, less time if they share a wall with a neighbor.

The dense colonies in which these swallows nest has led to a couple of interesting behavioral traits; many of the swallows are nest parasites and egg-smashers. In one study, up to 43 percent of nests contained at least one egg that did not belong to the nest owners. This happens in a couple of ways. First, a bird may enter a neighbor's nest and toss out an unguarded egg. Later, the parasite lays a replacement egg in the nest, or takes an egg from its own nest, carries it in its beak, and adds it to the neighbor's eggs. Cliff swallows cannot recognize their own eggs and they will incubate any egg they find in their nest.

After all the deceptions, each nesting pair usually hatches three chicks, and feeds them for three weeks until they fledge and leave the nest. The parents continue to feed the young by passing them food in flight for another four or five days, after which the young are left on their own.

Blue Jay

Cyanocitta cristata

Family Details
Crow, Jay, and Magpie Family, 117 species worldwide, 3 prairie species

This family of medium- to large-sized birds includes the bird brains, tricksters, and mimics of the avian world. They are among the most intelligent of birds, and many have phenomenal memories. A Clark's nutcracker, for example, may hide pine seeds in 2000 sites, in preparation for winter. Displaying a remarkable spatial memory, the nutcracker can then recall the 2000 locations for up to eight months afterwards.

Most of these birds are year-round residents and display great adaptability, especially in their diets. The birds have a sturdy, all-purpose bill that enables them to scavenge roadkills and the frozen carcasses of winter-killed animals; rob birds' nests; prey on frogs, snakes, and rodents; pluck berries from bushes; and pick ants and beetles from the ground.

These birds, collectively called corvids, generally have a loud, harsh voice, and their repertoire includes caws, croaks, squawks, and whistles. No one would confuse the noisy call of a corvid with the fluid music of a thrush or a warbler. Even so, the corvids are classified as songbirds, making the common raven the largest songbird in the world.

Field Identification
The jay is a robin-sized bird, bright blue above and smoky gray underneath. The bird has a prominent blue crest, a black necklace, and a large band of white on its folded wings.

Where to Find
The blue jay is a year-round resident in woodlands throughout the prairies, but it is most visible in winter when it forages around farms and suburban gardens and parks.

Wintering Grounds
The bright azure plumage of the blue jay is a welcome flush of color on a gray winter day. The jay is a regular winter patron at bird feeders. A band of these loquacious corvids will drive all the other birds away and control the feeder until they have eaten their fill of suet and seeds.

The blue color of the jay's feathers is an optical illusion resulting from their microscopic structure.

Diet and Feeding Habits

The blue jay, in common with most corvids, has a varied diet. It eats berries, seeds, acorns, beetles, grasshoppers, tent caterpillars, spiders, frogs, and salamanders. A notorious nest-robber, it was immortalized in a painting by the famous bird artist John James Audubon. Audubon wrote: "It [blue jay] imitates the cry of the sparrow hawk so perfectly that the little birds in the neighborhood hurry into thick coverts, to avoid what they believe to be the attack of that marauder. It robs every nest it can find, sucks the eggs like the crow, or tears to pieces and devours the young birds." The jay is a skilled mimic and can also imitate the calls of the red-tailed hawk, gray catbird, black-capped chickadee, northern oriole, American goldfinch, and others. It is still a mystery why the jay imitates so many birds.

The blue jay includes ants in its diet, but sometimes the bird uses the insects for something other than food. "Anting" is the preening behavior in which birds anoint their feathers with crushed or live ants. This unusual behavior has been described in nearly 200 species of birds, worldwide. Biologists speculate that the acrid formic acid secreted by ants, when wiped through a bird's feathers, may kill or discourage fleas, lice, mites, and other external parasites.

Breeding Biology

The blue jay builds a cup nest of twigs, bark, grass stems, lichens, paper, and feathers in the crotch of a tree, usually 3 to 4 meters (10–13 ft.) above the ground. The birds lay four or five pale green eggs, spotted with dark brown. The female incubates the eggs, but both parents aggressively defend the nest by dive-bombing and pecking intruders. House cats, dogs, and gray squirrels are common targets for their attacks. Anyone who has been scolded by a pair of angry blue jays knows that the noise alone is enough to drive you away. Young jays leave the nest when they are about three weeks old, and the parents continue to feed them for several weeks afterwards.

Trivia Tidbit

Birds can warm themselves by shivering, which is the repetitive involuntary contraction of a muscle. Birds such as the blue jay use the large chest muscles that power their wings as the major source of heat generated by shivering. On average, blue jays start shivering when the temperature drops to just 18°C (64°F). The gray jay, which lives farther north, is better adapted to cold temperatures. It begins shivering at 7°C (45°F).

Black-billed Magpie
Pica pica

Family Details

Crow, Jay, and Magpie Family, 117 species worldwide, 3 prairie species

See Blue Jay for a general discussion of the Crow, Jay, and Magpie Family.

Field Identification

The black-billed magpie is a crow-sized bird easily identified by its conspicuous black-and-white plumage and long tail. In the right light, the magpie's wings and tail shine iridescent greenish blue, making it a very beautiful bird indeed.

Where to Find

The magpie is common in suburban and farming areas throughout the prairies, but the bird is rarely seen in native grasslands.

Wintering Grounds

The magpie is a year-round resident of the prairies. In winter, the birds do not defend a territory, and travel widely over their home range in loose flocks of a dozen members or more. At night, 100 magpies may roost together in a cluster of trees or bushes.

Diet and Feeding Habits

Typically, the magpie feeds on the ground, hopping or walking with its long, handsome tail gracefully angled upwards. A foraging bird flicks litter with its bill, turns over dried cow-pies, and chases escaping insects on foot. Magpies eat mostly beetles, wasps, ants, and caterpillars. Its appetite for cutworms, wireworms, grasshoppers, and other insects harmful to crops should make these birds popular with any farmer or rancher. Still, in many rural areas the magpie is hated and persecuted.

After living on the prairies for 20 years, I've heard all the horror stories about magpies. How they supposedly peck out the eyes of sleeping lambs and calves, and eat the kidneys of live sheep by clinging tenaciously to the animals' backs. I've never seen the birds do these things, nor have any of the people who enthusiastically tell me these stories, but the tales are repeated nevertheless, and with each new telling the yarn is embellished and the magpies are maligned and shot. Certainly magpies do feed on carrion and winter-killed livestock, and the eyes of dead animals are often the first places they attack because they are easiest to eat. It's laughable, however, to believe that a sheep, no matter how dull-witted, would stand still and let its kidneys be eaten, or that a calf or lamb would not awaken when it was pecked in the eye by a magpie.

Breeding Biology

The black-billed magpie stays with the same partner for many years, often until one of them dies. The faithful pair probably builds the most distinctive nest of any prairie bird. The structure is a large, bulky, globular mass of thorny sticks, up to 8 meters (26 ft.) off the ground. The woven jumble may be more than a meter (3 ft.) in diameter, and take two months to complete. Two or three entrances lead inside, where the birds build a solid nest cup of mud, rootlets, grass stems, and wild animal hair in which to lay their eggs.

Magpies nest in small, loose colonies, often in the trees or bushes of a shelterbelt, a fence row, or a river valley. The sturdy nests are often refurbished and used for more than one season. Abandoned nests are recognizable for five or six years, and are used by many other prairie birds. Robins, bluebirds, and sparrows, for example, shelter inside them during bad weather, and many prairie kestrels, merlins, long-eared owls, mourning doves, and ducks use them to raise their young. The reason why magpies build such large, fortified nests is still unstudied. The nests may moderate extremes of temperature, or simply protect the owners and their eggs or nestlings from predators. The final answer awaits the scrutiny of a curious, bright-eyed graduate student.

The inside of a magpie nest can be extremely cramped and crowded. A pair may raise five to nine chicks, and they cluster inside the family fortress of sticks until they are almost a month old. By then there is barely room for a bird to blink. Once the youngsters escape to the outside world, they shadow their parents, scrounging and begging for one more month until the adults finally refuse to feed them another morsel.

Black-capped Chickadee

Parus atricapillus

Family Details
Titmouse Family, 53 species worldwide,
2 prairie species

Titmice are small, tame woodland songbirds. Most live in the Northern Hemisphere, where they are year-round residents of temperate and boreal forests, and as a result, must endure months of winter cold when food is hard to find. One way they survive such harsh environments is to store surplus food, hiding it under bits of bark, in knotholes, in the broken ends of twigs, and in tufts of conifer needles, retrieving it later when they are hungry. Tits in Norway, for example, may store between 50,000 and 80,000 spruce seeds each autumn.

Titmice use other ways to survive severe winter conditions. These energetic little birds are literally balls of fluff, and their plumage is much denser than that of other small songbirds. During the coldest weather, these birds will roost in small tree cavities or holes in the snow where their body heat warms the air around them and helps them to burn less energy. Many tits, especially chickadees, chill out at night, and let their body temperatures drop 10–12°C (18–22°F) below their normal daytime temperature of 40°C (104°F). The cooling can yield an energy saving of up to 23 percent, and may mean the difference between surviving a frigid night or succumbing to the cold.

Field Identification
The chickadee is a small, active bird with a black cap and bib, and white cheeks. In late winter, the distinctive *fee-bee* call of the chickadee may be the only bird song to interrupt the quiet cold of the prairie woods.

Where to Find
The black-capped chickadee is a common resident of wooded prairie coulees and river valleys, especially where there are groves of aspens.

Wintering Grounds
In winter, chickadees sometimes form temporary flocks with other resident birds. For example, half a dozen chickadees may travel with one or two downy woodpeckers, a red-breasted nuthatch, a white-breasted nuthatch, and a few kinglets and tree creepers. These "mixed feeding flocks" benefit the individuals in several ways. In such flocks, there are more eyes to detect danger, and the flight of a large group of birds is more likely to confuse a predator and foil its attack. As well, when different species of birds forage close together in a flock they can learn about new food sources from each other. For example, chickadees will often visit a site where a woodpecker was hammering to investigate what the bird found to eat.

Diet and Feeding Habits
The black-capped chickadee finds most of its food with three methods. More than half the time, the bird simply hops along small branches, searching the bark and leaves for scale insects, plant lice, and beetles. Less often it uses its strong legs to hang upside down like an acrobat on the underside of branches so it can locate hidden insects. Finally, the chickadee can hover and pluck caterpillars from the outermost leaves.

Chickadees will also eat the hairy caterpillars of the gypsy moth and the tent caterpillar moth, both of which are often rejected by other insectivorous birds. Veteran chickadee researcher Dr. Susan Smith has seen black-capped chickadees repeatedly tearing open the silken nests of tent caterpillars to feed on the juicy grubs.

The autumn and winter diet of the chickadee contains much less animal food. In these seasons of austerity, the birds commonly eat berries and seeds, especially the seeds of coniferous trees. They also scour the bark of trees and bushes to search for dormant insect eggs and hibernating spiders.

Breeding Biology
The chickadee nests in a tree cavity, which the pair excavates in the rotten wood of a limb, stump, or knothole. The inside of the cavity is well-lined with fur, feathers, fine strips of bark, moss, and plant down. In early May, the female lays six to nine speckled eggs and incubates them alone while her mate continues to feed her. The young hatchlings must be brooded continuously by the female until they are 12 days old and feathered enough to keep themselves warm. During this time, the "submissive" male continues to feed his "dominant" mate, as well as the young. The chicks fledge a few days later, and the family travels together for two to four weeks afterwards. Family breakup is abrupt, and all the youngsters disperse within one or two days.

Trivia Tidbit
The endearing little black-capped chickadee is the official avian ambassador of the states of Maine and Massachusetts, and the province of New Brunswick.

Page 110: The black-capped chickadee, literally a ball of fluff, relies on its thick plumage to shield it from the cold.

House Wren

Troglodytes aedon

Family Details

Wren Family, 75 species worldwide, 5 prairie species

The wrens are a family of small, chunky birds with slender, pointed bills and uptilted tails. The majority of these energetic little birds live in the tropics of Central and South America. The scientific name for the group is *Troglodytidae*, which is derived from the Greek for cave dweller or one who lives in dark, secret places. The name is well chosen since many wrens inhabit dense underbrush and reedy marshes where they hop and flit around, stealthily peer out, and then disappear again into the shadows.

Most wrens are plain brownish. This is not surprising, since bright, colorful plumage would be wasted in the dim, shadowed world in which these birds live. As a result, rather than use conspicuous plumage to signal each other and communicate, rival wrens use their voices, and many of them are superb singers with rich, complicated songs.

One of the most unusual behaviors seen among wrens is the habit that many males have of building "dummy nests." A male may build a dozen or more nests, only one of which will be used by his mate to lay her eggs. Some scientists speculate that the multiple nests may be an anti-predator strategy, the reasoning being that once a nest-robber checks a few nests and finds them empty it will stop looking and leave before it locates the real nest.

Field Identification

The house wren is one of those confusing LBJs— Little Brown Jobs—that exasperate birdwatchers. This brownish wren is smaller than a sparrow and often carries its tail cocked forward over its back. Its

This house wren is busy adding the final twigs to its nest in the hollow knothole of a cottonwood.

call is a delightful bubbling cascade of whistles that is not easily confused with the song of any other prairie bird.

Where to Find
The house wren is found in dense thickets throughout the prairies. This inquisitive little bird readily settles close to humans, and as its common name suggests, it will nest near houses and buildings if thick shrubbery is nearby for a retreat.

Wintering Grounds
This tiny wren, which weighs only 10 to 12 grams (0.4–0.5 oz.) when it is fattened up for its autumn migration, flies to the southern United States and Mexico for the winter. Most house wrens leave in August and early September and are back on the prairies by the middle of May.

Diet and Feeding Habits
The house wren may sometimes forage high in the foliage of a tree, but most often it hunts near the ground in dense shrubbery, exploring every nook and cranny for crickets, beetles, ticks, spiders, plant lice, ants, wasps, and bees. This small, pugnacious bird often punctures the eggs or kills the nestlings of bluebirds, tree swallows, and other house wrens. The wren never eats the eggs or chicks of its victims, and its killing instinct apparently is a strategy to lessen competition for nest sites, rather than to obtain food.

Breeding Biology
The male house wren defends a small territory and advertises his ardor by singing loudly and often. The house wren always nests in a cavity, but at times it ends up in rather unexpected locations. Besides the usual knotholes, old woodpecker holes, rock cavities, and crevices in trunks and broken snags, the wren may also settle inside the dried skull of a cow, in an old boot or shoe, in a flower pot, or in the tailpipe of an abandoned tractor. Typically the male builds several dummy nests of sticks and twigs and then waits for Lady Wren to make her choice and add the finishing touch: a fine lining of feathers, hair, and plant fibers. A pair of house wrens usually raises six to eight young, and they may set a feeding record doing it. According to author Frank Todd, the house wren may feed its young more frequently than any other bird in North America. In Todd's fascinating book *10,001 Titillating Tidbits of Avian Trivia* he writes that one male house wren returned to the nest 1,217 times within a 16.25-hour period, an average of one feeding visit every 47 seconds! The hard work ends when the wrenlets finally leave the nest between 14 and 18 days of age.

Marsh Wren
Cistothorus palustris

Family Details
Wren Family, 75 species worldwide, 5 prairie species
See House Wren for a general discussion of the Wren Family.

Field Identification
This brownish wren has a prominent white eye line and a whitish throat and underparts. The marsh wren lives in bulrushes and cattails, and this habit can be used to distinguish it from all other prairie

wrens except possibly the sedge wren, which at times may live in reedy marshes. The sedge wren differs in having buffy underparts and a streaked crown. If you have reached this level of birding skill you don't need me to help you, and I won't say another word.

This is one of four "dummy" nests a male marsh wren had built in its territory.

Where to Find
The wren is found in large cattail marshes and sloughs throughout much of the prairies.

Wintering Grounds

Marsh wrens leave in August to winter in the coastal marshes of the Gulf of Mexico, and in fresh and salt-water wetlands throughout Mexico. Most wrens are back calling in the cattails by early May.

Diet and Feeding Habits

The marsh wren is a spider's worst nightmare, and these eight-legged wolves are one of the bird's most common foods. The sharp-beaked little wrens also hunt beetles, bees, wasps, bugs, and moths. In their 1997 monograph *Marsh Wren*, authors Drs. Donald Kroodsma and Jared Verner wrote: "Foraging wrens are nearly always on the move, hopping and creeping among the bases of cattail stalks or threading their way through a tangle of fallen bulrush stems."

Breeding Biology

John James Audubon thought the marsh wren's rattling call resembled "the grating of a rusty hinge." Only male wrens sing, and these little testosterone-charged songsters really whistle. In western Nebraska, each male marsh wren sings an average of 211 different songs. Neighboring males commonly engage in vocal duels, imitating each other's songs and trying to outdo one another, and these long-winded singers chatter day and night. In a Manitoba marsh, the wrens called at night, between 1 AM and 3 AM, as often as they did during the day. Calling at night may lessen interference from other marsh-dwelling songbirds.

Male marsh wrens work while they whistle, building half a dozen dummy nests for every female partner they have, and some males may eventually mate with two or three partners. In a cattail marsh in Manitoba, 8 percent of the males were bachelors, 44 percent had a single mate, 40 percent were bigamists, and 8 percent were trigamists.

Marsh wrens build globe-shaped nests of cattails, sedges, and grasses, somewhat smaller than a football, and anchored to a dried cluster of cattail stalks. The male adds a lining of cattail down inside the nest, and later his female partner adds grasses, rootlets, and fine strips of marsh vegetation to the one she will use.

The wren lays a clutch of four to six pinkish-buff-colored eggs flecked with grayish brown scribbles and spots. The female incubates the eggs alone for 13 days, and provides most of the meals for the hatchlings. The male wren may, or may not, help to feed the chicks, and this varies among populations of marsh wrens. In the marshes of New York State, for example, no males fed their offspring, whereas in Manitoba nine out of 65 males brought food to their chicks, but only after the nestlings were eight days old. Despite such poor male participation, the male wrens that feed their chicks produce heavier nestlings and fledge more young than do absentee fathers.

At two weeks of age, young marsh wrens drop out of their cattail nests and scurry into cover. The young wrens are fed by one or both parents for a couple of weeks after they leave the nest.

The marsh wren is an agile acrobat, straddling grass stems and clinging to waving reeds with equal ease.

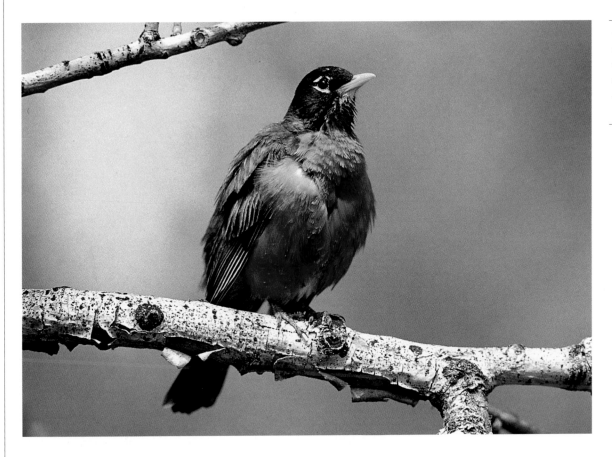

In a single day, a robin may catch enough earthworms to stretch 4.3 meters (14 ft.).

American Robin

Turdus migratorius

Family Details
Thrush Family,
179 species worldwide, 6 prairie species

The thrushes are a family of small- to medium-sized woodland songbirds. Many of them forage on the ground, where they use their strong legs to scratch in the leaf litter for insects and earthworms. A cryptic plumage of gray, brown, and white is common among the thrushes and camouflages them well in the mixture of light and shadow on the forest floor. Some thrushes, however, namely the bluebirds, are brightly colored and forage in the open, where their vibrant plumage flashes in the sunshine.

Thrushes are noted for their beautiful eggs. Among the North American species, almost all of them lay glossy greenish blue eggs, some of which are accented with rusty speckles and splotches. From a scientific standpoint, it's unclear why the eggs are so brightly colored. Regardless, the blue egg color of one of the thrushes is so striking and distinctive that it is now used as an accepted color standard: robin's egg blue.

Field Identification
The American robin is so familiar to everyone that it hardly needs to be described. The bird's distinctive rusty chest and belly reminded early British settlers of the English robin with its reddish face and breast, and the homesick colonists gave it the same name. The male and female American robin are similar except that the female's breast color is somewhat duller.

Where to Find
The robin is common in wooded river valleys and coulees throughout the prairies. The bird also adapts well to humans and frequently nests in farmyards and suburban gardens and parks.

Wintering Grounds
The American robin winters throughout the southern United States. The few that try to winter on the prairies invariably succumb to the cold. Every year in April, without fail, the local television station announces the first spring sighting of the robin in our area of the prairies. For most viewers, the cheery bird is the surest sign that summer is on the way.

Diet and Feeding Habits
In typical thrush fashion, the robin often forages on the ground, running for its meals. It hunts in

meadows, plowed fields, lawns, and golf courses, where it searches for wireworms, cutworms, beetles, ants, termites, and grasshoppers. Who has not seen a photograph of a plump-chested robin leaning back, tugging on an earthworm anchored in the soil and stretched to the breaking point? The final score in this familiar contest is always the same: Robins one, Earthworms zero. I always wondered how the robin located the earthworms in the first place. The birds often tilt their heads when they are hunting as if they are listening for prey to reveal itself. Researcher Frank Heppner solved the mystery in an erudite paper entitled "Sensory mechanisms and environmental clues used by the American robin in locating earthworms." Heppner's conclusion was that the robin finds worms in their burrows not by sound, but by sight. The robin simply cocks its head to improve its depth perception so that it can strike with greater accuracy.

In autumn, flocks of robins travel together and settle on berry bushes and fruit trees. In the prairies, their favorites include pin cherries, chokecherries, saskatoons, and rosehips, which they devour with equal relish.

Breeding Biology

Everyone wonders if the robins nesting in their yard are the same ones that nested there the year before. A pioneer study done in the 1940s determined that 74 percent of robins returned to within 16 kilometers (10 mi.) of their original homes. Since many robins live to be eight or nine years old, and some 15 years old, the robin nesting in your yard may very well be an old friend.

The female robin is an independent mother who builds the nest and incubates the eggs pretty well on her own. The nest is bulky and cup-shaped, made of coarse grasses, leaves, and rootlets cemented together with mud. It is usually less than 6 meters (20 ft.) off the ground on a ledge or tree limb. The female lays four unmarked, glossy eggs. Male robins do not feed their mates, so the female must balance her nest duties with the needs of everyday life. As a result, throughout the day, the female incubates in shifts lasting about three-quarters of an hour separated by a 10-minute break during which time she feeds herself, preens, and stretches.

Newly hatched robin chicks are blind and helpless. The linings of their mouths are bright lemon yellow, and they wave them instinctively any time an adult lands and jars the nest. The male helps his mate to feed the chicks, and once they fledge at two weeks of age he may continue to feed them for another week or 10 days while the female prepares to raise a second clutch of eggs.

Mountain Bluebird

Sialia currucoides

Family Details

Thrush Family, 179 species worldwide, 6 prairie species

See American Robin for a general discussion of the Thrush Family.

Field Identification

The male is cerulean blue above and pale sky blue underneath. In flight, no other prairie bird has such brilliant blue wings. The female is much less colorful, and has a grayish brown head and body with some blue in her wings, tail, and rump.

Where to Find

The mountain bluebird is a bird of the western prairies, where it inhabits badlands, sagebrush flats, grasslands, and the edges of wooded coulees. Nest boxes have encouraged these bold, beautiful birds to settle along roadways throughout the West.

Wintering Grounds

The mountain bluebird is the most migratory of the three species of bluebirds found in North America. Most of them winter in the southwestern United States or northwestern Mexico. They leave the northern prairies by the middle of September but return again towards the end of winter, usually in late March and early April. In most years, the males precede the females by several weeks.

Diet and Feeding Habits

The mountain bluebird is one of the most carnivorous of the thrushes, eating more insects and less fruit than most of them do. Typically it hunts from an elevated perch, or by hovering. When prey is sighted, the bluebird quickly flutters to the ground and grabs the hapless victim with its sharp-edged beak. The most common food items include crickets, spiders, grasshoppers, caterpillars, beetles, butterflies, and ants.

Breeding Biology

Male mountain bluebirds are highly aggressive, and they defend their nest territory with chases and aerial displays, in which rival males hover in front of each other and flash the intense blue in their plumage as they rapidly open and close their wings. If neither

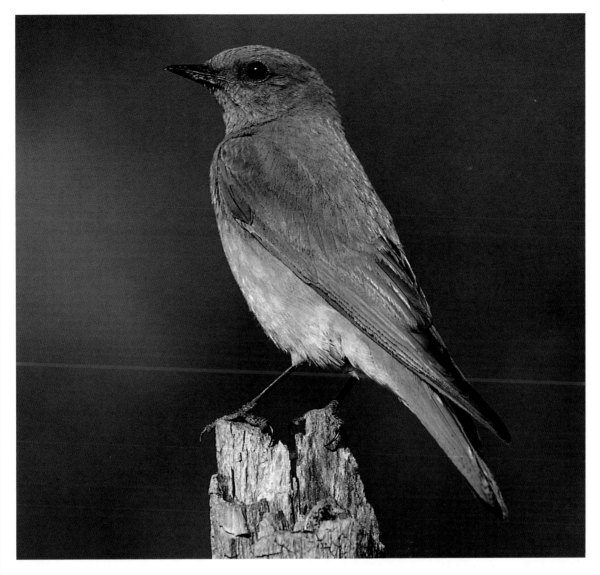

opponent is intimidated, hovering bluebirds may attack each other and grapple in flight. I once caught a male bluebird aggressively pecking its own reflection in the side mirror of my Jeep. The pugnacious bluebird returned to battle with this imaginary enemy half a dozen times in 15 minutes, even after I sat in the driver's seat directly beside the mirror.

Despite the vigilance of resident male bluebirds, intruders commonly trespass on their territories, and any of these male rivals could sneak a mating with their female partner. To prevent this, male mountain bluebirds guard their mates jealously throughout nest building and egg laying, when the female is most fertile. At these times, the male stays very close to his partner and never lets her out of his sight. This, in fact, is the only way the male can be certain that he will be feeding his own offspring rather than those of some dashing outsider.

Mountain bluebirds commonly nest in tree cavities, rock crevices, and bird houses. Such nest cavities are often in short supply, and many species may com-pete for them, including northern flickers, house wrens, house sparrows, and European starlings. In many of these house wars the bluebirds lose, and they are ousted, their eggs are destroyed, or their nestlings are murdered.

A bluebird family consists of five or six young, and the female broods the nestlings almost continuously until they are a week old. The hardworking male feeds both the female and the chicks. However, after a week, both parents bring caterpillars, grasshoppers, and spiders to the chicks, which grow quickly on this highly nutritious diet. Most chicks fledge between 18 and 21 days after hatching, but they continue to depend upon their parents to feed them for several weeks afterwards.

Two unexpected threats to bluebird nestlings come from insects and mammals. Stinging carpenter ants and blood-sucking blackflies may kill young chicks, and deer mice may take over the family nest, destroying the eggs and nestlings, even killing the adult female.

Eastern Bluebird

Sialia sialis

Family Details

Thrush Family, 179 species
worldwide, 6 prairie species

*See American Robin for a general discussion
of the Thrush Family.*

Field Identification

The male eastern bluebird is deep blue above with a
rusty throat, breast, and sides. The female is similar
but paler. The color in a bird's feathers is produced
either by pigments or by optical effects of light on the
microscopic structure of the feather. The intense blue
in the bluebirds is an optical illusion caused by the
structure of their feathers.

*During the final
week of chick
rearing, the male
eastern bluebird
may feed the
chicks alone.*

Where to Find

The eastern bluebird is restricted to the eastern half
of the prairies. This handsome songbird prefers forest
edges, and is seen less often in treeless habitats than is
the mountain bluebird. Like all of the bluebirds, the
eastern often associates with humans and may be
found around farmhouses and shelterbelts.

Wintering Grounds

Most eastern bluebirds winter in the southeastern
United States.

Diet and Feeding Habits

This bluebird commonly hunts in two ways: still-
hunting from a perch, and hover-hunting. In still-
hunting, the bird sits on an elevated perch, often a
fence wire or tree branch, and waits patiently for
unsuspecting prey to fly, hop, or scuttle by. From the
perch, the bluebird skillfully flies out to catch butterflies, wasps, and bees in midair, or dives to the
ground to capture grasshoppers, spiders, caterpillars,
beetles, ants, centipedes, and millipedes.

Hover-hunting can burn up to eight times more
energy than still-hunting, so the rewards need to
balance the energy costs. Bluebirds hover more often
when the wind is blowing strongly, and there is more
lift to the air. The birds also hover-hunt more when
they are feeding hungry young. In this instance, the
added cost of foraging is necessary to meet the nutritional needs of their offspring.

The bluebird, in common with most thrushes,
adds berries to its diet when the fruit ripens in the
late summer and autumn. When berries are plentiful,
bluebirds may gather in flocks of 100 or more to feed
together.

Breeding Biology

In bluebird courtship, the female sits and evaluates
while the male flutters and flashes. Typically, the
hopeful male suitor, while singing, fans his azure tail
and hovers in front of the perched female. It is likely
that the female can assess the health and vitality of
her prospective mate by the vigor of his hovering and
the brilliance of his plumage.

The eastern bluebird is a cavity-nester, as are all
bluebirds. Old woodpecker holes, crevices in tree
trunks, and hollows in stumps and old fenceposts are
popular natural nest sites. In the last 20 years, many
eastern bluebirds have moved into birdhouses built
specifically for them along "bluebird trails." Recent
innovations in the design of the birdhouses have less-
ened competition with other cavity-nesters, such as
tree swallows, wrens, house sparrows, and starlings,
all of whom covet the dry, snug birdhouses.

Potential nest cavities are often scarce, and the
male bluebird's territory centers around these valu-
able sites. Inside the nest cavity, the female weaves a
loose cup of grasses, feathers, and animal hair where
she lays four to six pale blue, glossy eggs. Incubation
and chick rearing take roughly six weeks. During the
final week or 10 days, the male may feed the chicks
alone while the female re-nests.

Trivia Tidbit

The handsome bluebird is an obvious choice as a
state bird. Idaho and Nevada use the mountain bluebird as their official avian ambassador, and the eastern bluebird is the Missouri and New York State bird.

Loggerhead Shrike

Lanius ludovicianus

Family Details

Shrike Family, 38 species worldwide, 2 prairie species

Shrikes warble and whistle, but they differ from other songbirds in one important way: they are predators with a taste for blood. Most shrikes are no larger than a robin, yet they hunt warblers, sparrows, bluebirds, and swallows, and capture them in mid-air. The predatory shrikes also prey on young ground squirrels, voles, mice, frogs, and lizards—even small, venomous rattlesnakes.

Shrikes are diurnal hunters with vision much better than that of humans. Their eyesight may be as good as that of sharp-eyed hawks and falcons. Raptor biologist Dr. Tom Cade had a pet northern shrike. The bird could spot a flying bumblebee 100 meters (328 ft.) away. At that distance the bee was invisible to Cade with his naked eye, but he could clearly see the insect with seven-power binoculars.

A mouse or a sparrow may be half the size of a shrike, so it would seem that the bird might sometimes tackle prey larger than it can handle. Not likely. A shrike has strong jaw muscles, and its hooked upper bill has a special wedge-shaped projection, called a tomial tooth, on each side just behind the tip. The tomial teeth, also found in falcons, are used by the shrike when it bites its victims on the neck to kill them.

A rapacious loggerhead shrike impales a dead deer mouse on a thorny branch of buckbrush.

Field Identification

The loggerhead shrike is a gray and white, robin-sized bird with a distinctive black mask and bill, and black tail. In flight, the shrike has black wings with a conspicuous white patch near the tips.

Where to Find

The shrike favors open pasturelands with scattered trees and shrubs. These birds frequently perch on fenceposts and telephone lines, and are often seen along roadsides. In the last 30 years, loggerhead shrikes have declined continent-wide because of poisoning from pesticides and because of the loss of shelterbelts, hedgerows, willow clumps, and trees to agriculture.

With such a large clutch of eggs, both adult logger-head shrikes must hunt to feed their chicks.

Wintering Grounds

Loggerhead shrikes from the northern prairies winter in Mexico and the southern United States.

Diet and Feeding Habits

In some areas, grasshoppers constitute 75 percent of a shrike's diet. The birds also eat beetles, wasps, bumblebees, butterflies, and spiders. Even though insects can be an important food for these birds, they have earned their reputation as rapacious predators because they hunt and kill anything that flutters, scampers, or scurries, including small rodents and many kinds of prairie songbirds.

The shrike, like many falcons, hawks, and eagles, hunts from a perch and captures its victims by a surprise attack from above. If the intended target escapes into a bush or long grass, the shrike does not abandon the chase; it simply jumps and hops about to flush its quarry into flight, where it can again be attacked.

Breeding Biology

Shrikes return to the prairies in early May. The birds are fiercely territorial and aggressively defend a small nesting territory. The scientific name for the loggerhead shrike is *Lanius ludovicianus*, which means "the butcher from Louisiana." The Louisiana portion of the name reflects the location of the first specimen described by science, but why is the bird called a butcher? It turns out that male shrikes commonly impale multiple prey items in the same bush or along the same stretch of barbed wire so that the area resembles a butcher shop. In one study, a researcher found a shrike larder containing 28 different prey items. The researcher emptied the larder and watched to see what the shrike would do. In two days, the larder had been restocked with 26 items. The size of a larder is a display of wealth and skill. A well-stocked larder advertises not only the quality of a male shrike's territory, but also his proficiency as a hunter and provider, and these attributes attract female shrikes.

The loggerhead shrike commonly builds its nest in thick, thorny shrubbery, such as buffaloberry and hawthorn. The female incubates alone and is fed by her mate for the 14 to 16 days it takes the eggs to hatch. The young fledge when they are around 17 days old. The parents continue to attack predators, such as bullsnakes, magpies, and crows, in defence of their offspring until the young are six weeks old and can fly well and feed themselves.

European Starling

Sturnus vulgaris

Family Details

Starling and Myna Family,
114 species worldwide, 1 prairie species

This is a family of stocky, medium-sized birds ranging in length from 15 to 40 centimeters (6–16 in.), many of them brightly colored in iridescent greens, blues, and purples. Most starlings and mynas live in the tropics of Africa, Asia, and the South Pacific, and none is native to the Americas. Two introduced species are found in North America, the crested myna and the familiar European starling. The ubiquitous starling was released in New York's Central Park in 1890 and 1891 in a misguided effort to introduce all of the birds mentioned in the writings of William Shakespeare.

The starlings and their relatives are renowned vocal mimics. For centuries, mynas in Asia have been kept as pets because of their ability to mimic human voices. The European starling is also no slouch when it comes to mimicry. Individual starlings may imitate the calls of 20 bird species, the most common being the American robin, killdeer, red-winged blackbird, meadowlark, northern flicker, and American crow. Ornithologists are uncertain of the biological purpose of mimicry, but it may be one way for a bird to enlarge its song repertoire, which is often a measure of the quality of a male suitor. In some species, mating success increases with increased repertoire size, and this may be ample reason for a starling to imitate all its neighbors.

Field Identification

The European starling is a year-round resident of the prairies. In late summer, autumn, and winter, the bird is black, finely speckled with white. In the breeding season, the speckles disappear and the starling is glossy black, all over, with green and purple iridescent highlights. Unlike most birds, which acquire their breeding plumage by replacing their feathers in a late winter molt, the starling loses its speckles by abrasion, gradually wearing away the white tips on its feathers.

After feeding the chicks, an adult European starling pauses unexplainably to scream at its young.

Where to Find

A hundred starlings were released in New York City in the late 1890s, and today they number over 200 million. These tough, adaptable birds were first sighted in prairie Alberta in 1934, and by 1970 they were breeding in Alaska. Starlings now occur continent-wide south of the treeline. Researcher Dr. Paul Cabe believes "[starlings] are arguably the most successful avian intruder to the continent." The European starling thrives especially well in agricultural and urban areas throughout the prairies.

Wintering Grounds

Starlings winter on the prairies. At the end of the breeding season, the birds gradually gather in flocks and roost together at night. The roosting flocks are largest in winter, and in some areas may contain more than a million birds.

Diet and Feeding Habits

Everyone has seen these chunky, square-tailed birds walking and running on their lawns searching for beetles, flies, caterpillars, grasshoppers, snails, earth-worms, and spiders. Although starlings prefer invertebrates when they are available, the versatile birds also eat grain, livestock feed, berries, fruits, and garbage. Their diverse diet partly explains why some people call them "rats with wings."

Breeding Biology

Male starlings usually mate with a single partner, but in some populations they pair with a second female. Second mates receive little help in incubating their eggs or feeding the young, and as a result, they fledge fewer chicks than do primary mates.

Starlings commonly nest in cavities found in buildings, in unused woodpecker holes, and in nest boxes. They are surprisingly aggressive in evicting other species from such cavities. Flickers, tree swallows, and bluebirds are frequent victims of these nest pirates. Once starlings claim a site, they fill the cavity with an untidy mix of grasses, rootlets, feathers, paper, string, and bits of plastic garbage. The usual clutch is five to seven pale blue eggs, which both parents incubate. The eggs hatch after two weeks, and the young fledge when they are three weeks old. Although the young may follow their parents and beg for food for several weeks afterwards, they are rarely fed for more than a few days after they leave the nest.

The black beak and white speckled plumage identifies this starling as a winter bird.

Yellow Warbler

Dendroica petechia

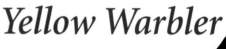

Family Details

Wood Warbler Family, 115 New World species, 27 prairie species

The wood warblers live only in the Americas, and are a group of small, delicate songbirds that flutter and flit among the leaves of shrubs and trees. They have slender, pointed bills, which they use to pick insects off vegetation. Half a dozen different species of warblers may forage in the same tree at the same time. They lessen competition by masterfully partitioning the habitat, feeding at different levels in the tree and at different distances from the trunk.

Most warblers are much smaller than sparrows, and they are often overlooked because of their tiny size and their habit of hunting quietly in the treetops and in shrubbery. On closer inspection, however, the males of many warbler species are colorfully feathered during the breeding season, and like flowers on the wing, these handsome little birds brighten any spring day.

The beautiful yellow warbler is the most widespread and common warbler in the prairies.

Field Identification

The yellow warbler is sometimes called the "wild canary," and is the only small all-yellow bird found in the prairies. The male has delicate rusty streaks on his breast and belly. This beautiful little songster might be confused with the similar-sized goldfinch, but the finch has a conspicuous black cap, wings, and tail.

Where to Find

The yellow warbler is one of the most widely distributed wood warblers in North America, and ranges from the Arctic treeline to the Rio Grande in Texas. In the prairies, the warbler is found in thickets of shrubbery along waterways, and in moist areas at the edges of woodlands.

Wintering Grounds

The yellow warbler, like all insect-eating songbirds, flees from the prairies in winter, as it would quickly succumb to the cold if it were to stay. Many leave in August and migrate to Mexico and Central America, although some yellow warblers may fly as far south as Brazil.

Diet and Feeding Habits

The warbler often hunts close to the ground, searching in shrubbery on the underside of leaves and stems for hiding insects. Although caterpillars may comprise more than two-thirds of their diet, the warblers also eat moths, bark beetles, damselflies, aphids, and grasshoppers. Warblers, along with many other insect-eating songbirds, use leaf damage to focus their foraging efforts and help them locate caterpillars more easily. In this deadly contest of hide-and-seek, many edible caterpillars lessen their chances of being eaten by feeding at night, by trimming the eaten leaves to make them less conspicuous to birds, and by hiding at sites away from the damaged leaves, where they are less likely to be found.

Breeding Biology

The female yellow warbler is remarkably tame as she builds the family nest over a three- to four-day period, and I once watched one of them at close range in a clump of willows. The nest was just a meter (3 ft.) off the ground, and consisted of a compact cup of dry grass stems, plant down, and feathers nestled in a crotch joining several branches. Some female warblers also use spider silk or the silken nests of tent caterpillars to bind the nest materials together.

Yellow warblers are usually monogamous, and the female builds her nest in the middle of the defended territory of her sweet-singing mate. The bird typically lays four or five white or light greenish eggs, speckled with dark brown, and she alone incubates the clutch for the 11 days it takes before the family hatches. Young warblers, like all songbird chicks, are ugly little wobbly-necked critters with huge, red mouths rimmed in bright yellow—a target that is hard to miss for a feeding parent. Both adults feed the hungry chicks, which leave the nest before they are two weeks of age.

The yellow warbler is a frequent victim of the brown-headed cowbird, which lays its eggs in the nests of other birds and then lets the foster parents raise the young for them. In many cases, when a warbler discovers a cowbird egg in its nest it may desert the nest, or simply bury the entire clutch in nest materials and then lay a replacement clutch on top. Even so, yellow warblers are still the main songbird chosen by parasitic cowbirds.

Red-winged Blackbird

Agelaius phoeniceus

Family Details

Blackbird and Oriole Family, 97 New World species, 11 prairie species

This family of medium-sized songbirds includes many popular species: the western meadowlark, whose fluid songs enliven the prairie landscape; the widespread red-winged blackbird, possibly the most abundant songbird in North America; and the resplendent orange-and-black northern oriole, one of the most striking birds. For such a relatively small family, the blackbirds and orioles display a surprising variety of nesting habits. Some species cradle their eggs in pendulous nests high in the treetops, while others hide them on the ground. Many are solitary,

A dominant male red-winged blackbird may mate with more than a dozen females.

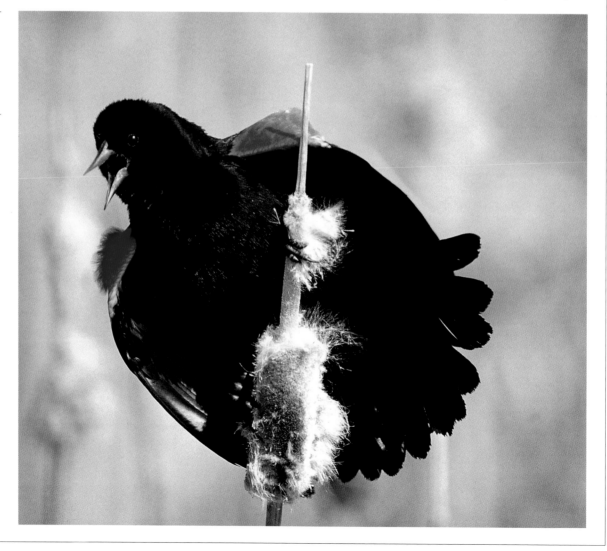

but some cluster in dense colonies in cattail marshes. And while most members of this family tirelessly care for their eggs and chicks, some cowbirds lay hundreds of eggs in their lifetime but never raise a single young. Instead, they lay their eggs in the nests of dozens of other birds and let the parasitized foster parents labor on their behalf.

Field Identification
The male red-winged blackbird is glossy black with bright red shoulder patches. The female has a mottled brown back with heavy streaking on her undersides.

Where to Find
Red-wings are most common in cattail marshes, although they readily settle in hayfields, pastures, roadside ditches, and urban wetlands of every description.

Wintering Grounds
Red-winged blackbirds migrate to the southern United States. Most leave the prairies rather late in the season, departing in October. The birds often winter in grain-producing areas, where they may mix with cowbirds, starlings, and grackles and form immense winter flocks, sometimes numbering several million birds. These familiar blackbirds return to the prairies in April.

Diet and Feeding Habits
Red-wings typically forage on the ground by walking and probing the vegetation and the surface layers of the soil. For much of the year, the birds eat mostly seeds and grains, but on their prairie breeding grounds their tastes turn to animal foods, such as caterpillars, flies, spiders, aquatic beetles, and damselflies. One afternoon I watched a brightly colored male red-wing feed his chicks lime-green caterpillars. The vibrancy and contrast of colors was hard to believe.

Breeding Biology
A male red-winged blackbird defends his territory with songs, aerial chases, and occasional grappling, wing-beating, bill-pecking battles. The bird's scarlet epaulets are important signals of dominance and ownership. When inquisitive scientists blackened the red shoulder patches on a group of males, more than half of them immediately lost their territories to intruders.

Red-wings are polygamous, and most males attract at least five female mates to their territory, and some "supermales" may lure up to 15 partners. A male has little hope of mating without a territory, so competition is intense. A red-wing may live for 14 years, an exceptional lifespan for a songbird. A long life is advantageous, since a male may wait years before he finally has a chance to breed. Roughly 50 percent of males secure a territory by three years of age, but some may be five years old before they finally own some real estate.

A male red-wing's territory may be as large as half a football field, and it is a constant challenge for him to guard his partners from outside suitors. In fact, he almost always fails. DNA fingerprinting has shown that up to 48 percent of the offspring raised in a male's territory are fathered by another male, usually one of his neighbors.

Each female red-wing builds her own nest, a woven cup of decayed leaves, roots, and mud suspended amongst several cattail stalks, 20 to 80 centimeters (8–31 in.) above the water. In the 1930s, a patient biologist dissected a red-wing nest to see how it was made. The nest was composed of 142 strips of cattail leaves, 34 strips of willow bark, and 705 pieces of grass. The philandering males never help their mates with nest building or incubation. Even after the chicks hatch, some males never feed their offspring, but when they do help, the fledglings are heavier and more of them survive.

Young red-wings leave the nest after two weeks, and the parents may feed them for up to five weeks afterwards. Once they are independent, the youngsters join mixed flocks of juveniles and adults, and forage and roost with the group until they migrate in the autumn.

Yellow-headed Blackbird
Xanthocephalus xanthocephalus

Family Details
Blackbird and Oriole Family,
97 New World species, 11 prairie species

See Red-winged Blackbird for a general discussion of the Blackbird and Oriole Family.

Field Identification
The yellow-head is a medium-sized blackbird of which the male is nearly twice as heavy as the female. Males are glossy black with a striking orange-yellow head, neck, and breast. In flight, the handsome male displays conspicuous white wing patches. Female yellow-heads are an overall brownish colour with a pale yellow chest and throat. The yellow chest and

The vibrancy of color in most birds, as in this male yellow-head, is a measure of health and vitality.

absence of prominent streaking in the female is the best way to distinguish her from the female red-wing, with which she is sometimes confused.

Where to Find
The yellow-headed blackbird is found throughout the prairies in sloughs, ponds, and lakes wherever there are cattails and bulrushes growing in relatively deep water.

Wintering Grounds
Yellow-heads winter in the southern United States and Mexico. The bird is less tolerant of cold than the red-winged blackbird, and it migrates a month or so sooner, leaving the prairies in late August and early September. The bird's intolerance to cold also delays its spring return; most yellow-heads arrive back on the prairies in the early days of May.

Diet and Feeding Habits
The versatile yellow-head may forage in marshes, croplands, plowed fields, and native prairies. In wetland habitats, the bird hops and climbs between the stalks of vegetation, gleaning aquatic invertebrates such as dragonfly and damselfly nymphs, diving beetles, and spiders from the water surface and the plants. In drier habitats, it feeds on cutworms, army worms, ground beetles, fly larvae, caterpillars, weed seeds, and grains.

Breeding Biology
Male yellow-heads often group their territories together, so the birds appear to be somewhat colonial. Within a stretch of cattails or bulrushes, each male defends his own bit of turf, advertising his ownership with an elaborate display performed from an exposed perch. The rivals fan their tails, spread and droop their wings to expose the white patches, and point their beaks skyward. Then, with all the gusto their hormone-charged bodies can muster, they rattle and growl the most unmusical of calls.

In many sloughs and marshes, yellow-headed blackbirds often share the wetland with red-winged blackbirds. Both birds eat similar foods, so there is a potential for competition. As a result yellow-heads, which are the larger of the two species, generally dominate red-wings, sometimes completely usurping the smaller birds' territories or relegating them to the margins of the marsh, where the water is shallower. On the edges of prairie wetlands, there is a greater danger from mammalian predators such as skunks, mink, red foxes, and deer mice, which prey on blackbird eggs and nestlings. Even with the protection of deeper water, as many as 48 percent of yellow-head nests are destroyed by predators before the chicks fledge.

Yellow-heads are polygamous, and the most charismatic of males may lure up to eight females into his territory, although a harem of three or four is more typical. The females do most of the household duties. They build the nest, incubate the three or four eggs, and brood the chicks when they hatch as big-eyed, wrinkled blobs of life. After four or five days, the male yellow-head finally rises to the challenge of fatherhood and begins to help feed his offspring. He pays most attention to the first of his mates, however, and offers less help to the subordinate females in his harem.

When blackbird chicks first leave the nest at two weeks of age, they can only hop among the stalks of their cattail world. Within a week, they can flutter a meter or two (3–6 ft.), and by three weeks of age they can flap for 25 meters (82 ft.) or more. Chicks of this age often shadow their parents closely, and noisily beg for food. The free lunches end soon afterwards.

Male yellow-heads must constantly chase trespassers from their territory to prevent matings with their resident females.

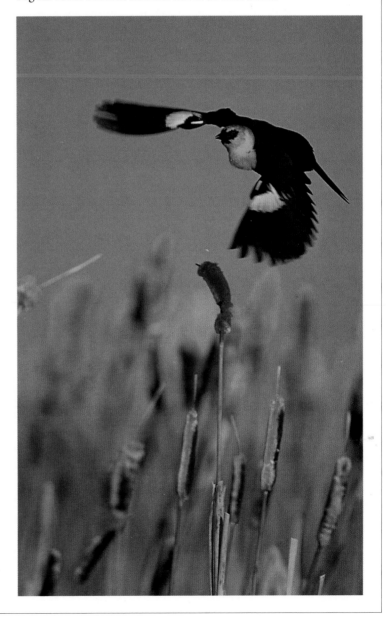

Western Meadowlark

Sturnella neglecta

Family Details

Blackbird and Oriole Family,
97 New World species, 11 prairie species

See Red-winged Blackbird for a general discussion of the Blackbird and Oriole Family.

Field Identification

The meadowlark is familiar to most prairie residents and hardly needs to be described. It is a medium-sized bird with bright yellow underparts emblazoned with a black V across its upper breast. The male and female are similar in appearance, although the female tends to be less brightly colored. In flight, the bird's white outer tail feathers are conspicuous.

Where to Find

The western meadowlark is common and widespread in fields, pastures, and native grasslands throughout the prairies. The bird prefers open areas and rarely enters woodlands.

Wintering Grounds

In the central and southern prairies, the meadowlark is a year-round resident. But in the cold northern prairies, the birds migrate south into the United States and northern Mexico for the winter.

Diet and Feeding Habits

The meadowlark feeds mainly on the ground, where it probes the soil with its wedge-shaped bill searching for fly larvae, ants, weevils, beetles, and cutworms. It also searches under clods of dried manure for crickets and dung beetles. The omnivorous meadowlark also eats grain, weed seeds, and fruit, and occasionally preys on the eggs and young of other ground-nesting songbirds.

Breeding Biology

Adult males return to the prairies in April, two to four weeks before the females, and immediately begin their melodious dusk and dawn concerts from the tops of fenceposts, wild rose bushes, and clumps of sagebrush. The bird's delightful flute-like song bubbles across the prairies.

A territorial male may sing as many as six to nine song types, attempting to outdo his neighbors and lure a mate with an ear for quality. In a contest between neighboring songsters, a male may run through his entire repertoire, switching songs whenever his rivals do. Studies show that males with larger repertoires, which may signal the superior quality of the singer, attract a mate earlier and raise more young than do their vocally challenged competitors. Clearly, in the world of the meadowlark, the silver-tongued lover lures the most ladies.

The competition among rival males is not limited to vocal duelling. Veteran meadowlark researcher Dr. Wesley Lanyon wrote: "Body contact and fighting between males, though uncommon, can be quite severe with much thrashing of wings, jabbing of bills, and clawing. One combat lasted three minutes, during which the two males grappled so intently they tumbled awkwardly about on the ground."

More than half of the male western meadowlarks entice two females to nest simultaneously in their territory, and a few males lure three. The birds nest on the ground, and although the nests are well concealed in thick grass, predators discover many of them. Common egg-nappers include skunks, coyotes, foxes, magpies, and crows. I learned firsthand about one of the more unusual predators. When I first found the nest, it held four fuzz-covered chicks. I left it undisturbed and returned two days later to take a family portrait. When I parted the grass covering the brood, the nest was empty. I felt sick, and for an instant I blamed myself for the loss, believing my scent had attracted a predator. I parted the grass farther to examine the nest more closely, and there it was: a large prairie rattlesnake bulging from its most recent meal. The snake had eaten all of the nestlings. I took a quick mugshot of the culprit and then left it to digest its dinner in peace.

With so many predators scouring the prairie, it makes sense for meadowlark chicks to leave home as soon as they can, and the young fledge when they are just 10 to 12 days old. At this age, the youngsters have strong legs to run quickly and hide, but their flight feathers are not fully developed and they cannot fly. The young depend upon their parents to feed them for another two weeks while they grow and become independent.

Trivia Tidbit

The western meadowlark is the official state bird of Kansas, Montana, Nebraska, North Dakota, Oregon, and Wyoming, more states than any other bird.

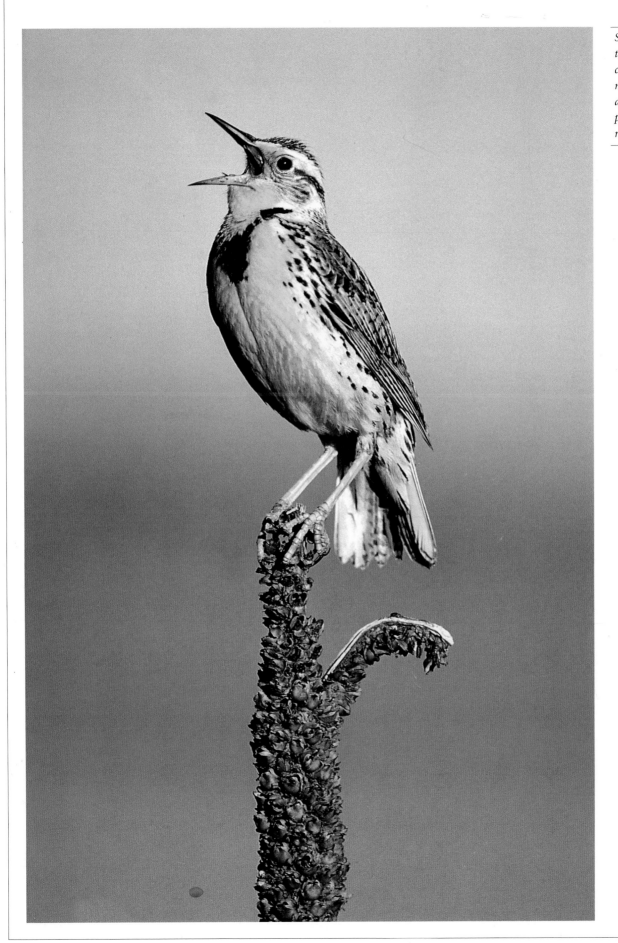

House Sparrow

Passer domesticus

Family Details

Old World Sparrow Family, 36 species worldwide, 1 prairie species

This is a small family of songbirds, most of whom live in Africa and India. All of the sparrows are seed-eating birds with short, conical bills adapted to crushing tough foods. One of the family, the familiar house sparrow, was systematically introduced into North and South America, southern Africa, Australia, and New Zealand, and has become one of the most successful avian colonists on Earth.

The story of the sparrow's introduction into North America is well known. In the spring of 1853, Nicholas Pike released a large number of these birds into Greenwood Cemetery in New York City. In the next two decades, other misguided bird lovers released the sparrows throughout New England, the Midwest, parts of eastern Canada, and California, Texas, and Utah. In less than 100 years the bird colonized most of the continent—the fastest avian conquest ever recorded.

This male house sparrow was part of a spring flock of 30 birds feeding on spilled grain beside an elevator.

Field Identification

The male house sparrow is a small, brownish bird with a gray cap, chestnut nape, black bib, and white cheeks. The black bib is present only during the breeding season. The female sparrow looks the same year-round, and is plain brown with a streaked back.

Where to Find

Although the house sparrow ranges throughout the continent from Arctic tundra to deserts and prairies, the bird occurs almost solely in association with humans and their buildings, and is rarely seen elsewhere. In the prairies, large numbers of house sparrows live around grain elevators and farm buildings, and are a common sight in every town and city.

Wintering Grounds

The tough little house sparrow winters on the prairies. The birds vary in size throughout the continent depending upon the climate; the largest sparrows live in the coldest climates. As a result, northern prairie house sparrows weigh more and have larger bodies than their relatives living farther south. The sparrows can endure temperatures colder than -20°C (-4°F), but to do so they rely heavily on their fat reserves and a sheltered roost.

Diet and Feeding Habits

Looking at the stout conical beak of the house sparrow you could predict that the bird is a seed eater. Spilled grain, and grass and weed seeds are their main diet. These birds, however, did not become as widespread as they are without a good measure of dietary flexibility. The adaptable house sparrow also eats beetles, grasshoppers, and weevils. They sometimes hunt flying insects attracted to lights at night, they will pierce flowers to steal the nectar, and I have often seen them scavenge dead insects from the front grill of my Jeep.

Breeding Biology

The size of the black bib on the male house sparrow is a signal of rank, and the larger the bib the higher the bird's rank and the greater his attractiveness to females. Since high-ranking males breed earlier and claim the best nest sites, why do male sparrows not simply cheat the system and grow larger bibs? The size of the bib is controlled by the male hormone testosterone. In sparrows, high testosterone levels have a serious side-effect: they suppress the bird's immune system, making them more prone to parasites and shortening their lifespan. Clearly, in house sparrows, the sexiest males pay a high price for their charisma.

High-ranking male sparrows commonly claim a nest site in autumn and control it all winter until the breeding season begins in April. House sparrows typically nest in cavities, and choose nooks and crannies in buildings and nestboxes. Sparrows are aggressive and will displace swallows, purple martins, and bluebirds from nestboxes, sometimes killing their rivals and building a nest over the bodies of the former owners. Typically, the birds build a domed nest of dried stems, feathers, string, and bits of cloth and paper. The female lays three to five greenish white eggs variably marked with dark spots and speckles. The monogamous pair shares the two-week incubation of the eggs, and takes turns brooding the hatchlings until they are six days old and can keep themselves warm. Both parents feed the chicks regurgitated insects for the two weeks of nest life and for seven to ten days afterwards. The independent youngsters join flocks of other juveniles that roost and forage together.

Common Redpoll

Carduelis flammea

Family Details
Finch Family, 140 species
worldwide, 10 prairie species

The finches are a group of small to medium-sized seed-cracking specialists. Although many birds eat seeds some of the time, most switch to softer fruits and insects when they are available. Finches, on the other hand, eat seeds all of the time, and the shape of

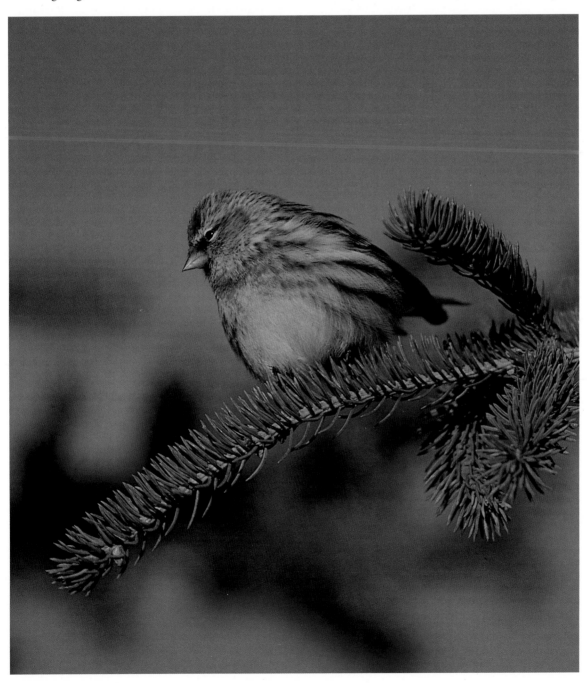

The plucked body of a redpoll is the size of a man's thumb, which makes it the smallest bird wintering on the prairies.

their beaks illustrates how well-adapted these birds are to this type of food. Whereas blue jays and chickadees hammer seeds until they split, and grouse and mourning doves swallow them whole and grind them up in their muscular gizzards, most finches simply bite down hard with their powerful beaks until the seed cracks. The beak and jaws of a grosbeak, for example, are so strong that they can crush the hardest seeds, even cherry pits.

The finch family includes many species that normally live year round in the boreal forest and the Arctic. These hardy birds can endure extreme cold if they have enough seeds to fuel their internal furnaces. When seed crops fail in the northern forests, as they do on a regular basis every two or three years, the birds have no option but to flee southward in winter to search for food. These periodic finch invasions, called irruptions, are eagerly awaited by prairie birdwatchers.

Field Identification
The common redpoll is a small, streaked, tan and white bird with a bright crimson forehead. In late winter, the male's breast is flushed with rosy pink as if it had been dipped in strawberry juice. The birds commonly travel in flocks.

Where to Find
Flocks of these beautiful finches may sometimes be flushed along roadsides in winter as they forage for weed seeds. However, they most often invade towns and cities, where they cluster in birch trees and at bird feeders.

Wintering Grounds
The common redpoll and its close relative, the hoary redpoll, are winter visitors to the prairies. Weighing about 14 grams (0.5 oz.), the redpoll is one of the smallest birds to winter here. It survives the rigorous climate by tunnelling at night into the snow, where the temperature may be 22°C (40°F) warmer than the outside air. This resourceful little finch has another trick to get through the night. It chills out—literally. At night, a redpoll may let its body temperature drop by as much as 10°C (18°F), earning the bird a substantial saving of energy.

Diet and Feeding Habits
The redpoll eats the small seeds of many northern plants, including willows, alders, and poplars, but its favorite food is birch seeds. At the end of each winter day, the bird commonly stores extra food, particularly birch seeds, in a specialized pouch in its esophagus. During the night, when the redpoll is roosting, it can regurgitate the seeds if it needs extra energy. Researchers found that once a redpoll had filled up

on birch seeds, it could survive a night when the temperature dropped to -62°C (-80°F). Without access to the calorie-rich seeds, however, the bird's limit was -30°C (-22°F).

Breeding Biology
The female redpoll builds a delicate cup nest of rootlets, grasses, and mosses, one to two meters (3–6.5 ft.) high in an alder or willow bush. The nest is often lined with ptarmigan feathers, which insulate it against the predictable cold of a northern spring. The birds lay four or five beautiful pale blue eggs spotted with lilac and reddish brown scrawls and speckles. The drabbly colored female incubates the eggs alone, but both parents feed the young until they leave the nest at two weeks of age.

Pine and Evening Grosbeaks

Pinicola enucleator and Coccothraustes vespertinus

Family Details
Finch Family, 140 species worldwide, 10 prairie species

See Common Redpoll for a general discussion of the Finch Family.

Field Identification
Both species of grosbeaks are plump, medium-sized birds with large, conical bills. The male pine grosbeak has a dark red head, breast, back and rump, and the female has a gray body with a yellowish head and rump. Both sexes have dark wings and tails. The male evening grosbeak is easy to distinguish with its yellow body, brighter yellow eyebrow, and dark brown head. The female evening grosbeak is grayish tan with a white-tipped dark tail. Both sexes have a white patch on each dark wing.

Where to Find
The grosbeaks inhabit many prairie towns and cities during the cold winter months. They are popular visitors at winter bird feeders.

Wintering Grounds
Both species of grosbeaks are strictly winter visitors. Usually these beautiful birds arrive on the prairies in late autumn, and leave in April or May to migrate

*To stay warm in winter,
pine grosbeaks fluff up their
feathers to increase the
insulating layer of trapped air.*

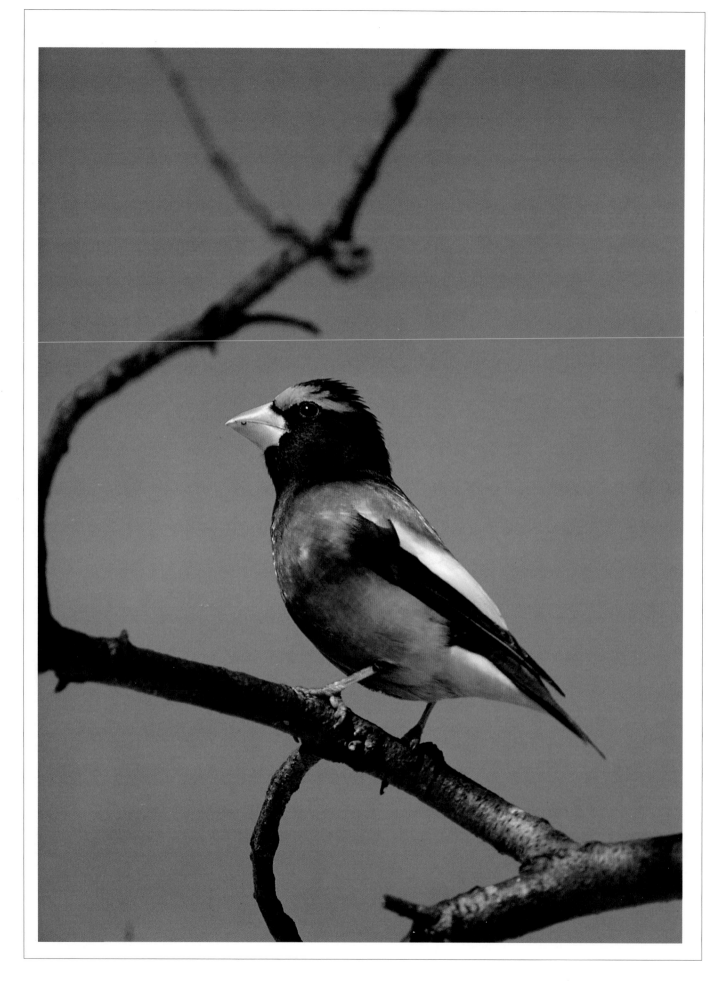

north to their nesting grounds in the boreal forest. Grosbeaks are extremely gregarious and commonly travel in flocks of a dozen or two, and sometimes a group may number 100 birds or more. Pine and evening grosbeaks usually do not flock together, although they may gather at the same bird feeder.

Diet and Feeding Habits

In winter, these birds devour great numbers of sunflower seeds at bird feeders. Pine grosbeaks also feed on mountain ash berries, crabapples, and the seeds of spruce trees and Manitoba maples. Evening grosbeaks eat less fruit and concentrate more on the seeds of green ash, Manitoba maple, box elder, and paper birch. In spring, both birds eat the swelling buds of aspens and willows.

Breeding Biology

Both of these handsome seed crackers nest in northern coniferous forests. The females of both grosbeaks usually build a loose cup nest of roots, twigs, mosses, and lichens high in a spruce or fir tree. Each lays a clutch of three or four eggs, which are incubated entirely by the female while her faithful mate dutifully brings her meals of beetles, caterpillars, grasshoppers, flies, cankerworms, and spruce budworms. The same appetizing meals are fed to the hatchlings by both parents until the young leave the nest at roughly two weeks of age.

Page 134: The massive beak of the evening grosbeak identifies it as the premier seed-cracker on the prairies.

American Birding Association – Code of Ethics

We, the Membership of the American Birding Association, believe that all birders have an obligation at all times to protect wildlife, the natural environment, and the rights of others. We therefore pledge ourselves to provide leadership in meeting this obligation by adhering to the following general guidelines of good birding behavior.

1. **Birders must always act in ways that do not endanger the welfare of birds or other wildlife.**

In keeping with this principle, we will:

♦ Observe and photograph birds without knowingly disturbing them in any significant way.

♦ Avoid chasing or repeatedly flushing birds.

♦ Only sparingly use recordings and similar methods of attracting birds and not use these methods in heavily birded areas.

♦ Keep an appropriate distance from nests and nesting colonies so as not to disturb them or expose them to danger.

♦ Refrain from handling birds or eggs unless engaged in recognized research activities.

2. **Birders must always act in ways that do not harm the natural environment.**

In keeping with this principle, we will:

♦ Stay on existing roads, trails, and pathways whenever possible to avoid trampling or otherwise disturbing fragile habitat.

♦ Leave all habitat as we found it.

3. **Birders must always respect the rights of others.**

In keeping with this principle, we will:

♦ Respect the privacy and property of others by observing "No Trespassing" signs and by asking permission to enter private or posted lands.

♦ Observe all laws and the rules and regulations that govern public use of birding areas.

♦ Practice common courtesy in our contact with others. For example, we will limit our requests for information, and we will make them at reasonable hours of the day.

♦ Always behave in a manner that will enhance the image of the birding community in the eyes of the public.

4. **Birders in groups should assume special responsibilities.**

As group members, we will:

♦ Take special care to alleviate the problems and disturbances that are multiplied when more people are present.

♦ Act in consideration of the group's interest, as well as our own.

♦ Support by our actions the responsibility of the group leader(s) for the conduct of the group.

As group leaders, we will:

♦ Assume responsibility for the conduct of the group.

♦ Learn and inform the group of any special rules, regulations, or conduct applicable to the area or habitat being visited.

♦ Limit groups to a size that does not threaten the environment or the peace and tranquility of others.

♦ Teach others birding ethics by our words and example.

Courtesy of the American Birding Association

Checklist

Species	Date first sighted
Grebe Family	
❏ Red-necked Grebe	
❏ Eared Grebe	
❏ Horned Grebe	
❏ Pied-billed Grebe	
Pelican Family	
❏ American White Pelican	
Cormorant Family	
❏ Double-crested Cormorant	
Waterfowl Family	
❏ Northern Pintail	
❏ Mallard	
❏ American Wigeon	
❏ Northern Shoveler	
❏ Blue-winged Teal	
❏ Cinnamon Teal	
❏ Redhead and Canvasback	
❏ Ruddy Duck	
❏ Canada Goose	
❏ Snow Goose	
❏ Tundra Swan	
❏ Trumpeter Swan	
New World Vulture Family	
❏ Turkey Vulture	
Hawk and Eagle Family	
❏ Golden Eagle	
❏ Bald Eagle	
❏ Northern Harrier	
❏ Ferruginous Hawk	
❏ Swainson's Hawk	
❏ Red-tailed Hawk	

Species	Date first sighted
Falcon and Caracara Family	
❏ Prairie Falcon	
❏ American Kestrel	
❏ Peregrine Falcon	
Grouse Family	
❏ Ruffed Grouse	
❏ Sharp-tailed Grouse	
❏ Sage Grouse	
Partridge and Pheasant Family	
❏ Ring-necked Pheasant	
Heron Family	
❏ American Bittern	
❏ Great Blue Heron	
❏ Black-crowned Night-heron	
Crane Family	
❏ Sandhill Crane	
Rail Family	
❏ American Coot	
Avocet and Stilt Family	
❏ Black-necked Stilt	
❏ American Avocet	
Snipe, Sandpiper, and Phalarope Family	
❏ Wilson's Phalarope	
❏ Long-billed Curlew	
❏ Willet	
❏ Upland Sandpiper	
❏ Marbled Godwit	
Plover Family	
❏ Killdeer	
❏ Piping Plover	

Species	Date first sighted	Species	Date first sighted
Gull Family		**Crow, Jay, and Magpie Family**	
❏ California Gull		❏ Blue Jay	
❏ Ring-billed Gull		❏ Black-billed Magpie	
❏ Franklin's Gull		**Titmouse Family**	
Tern Family		❏ Black-capped Chickadee	
❏ Forster's Tern		**Wren Family**	
❏ Black Tern		❏ House Wren	
Pigeon and Dove Family		❏ Marsh Wren	
❏ Mourning Dove		**Thrush Family**	
Owl Family		❏ American Robin	
❏ Long-eared Owl		❏ Mountain Bluebird	
❏ Great Horned Owl		❏ Eastern Bluebird	
❏ Short-eared Owl		**Shrike Family**	
❏ Burrowing Owl		❏ Loggerhead Shrike	
❏ Northern Saw-whet Owl		**Starling and Myna Family**	
❏ Snowy Owl		❏ European Starling	
Nightjar Family		**Wood Warbler Family**	
❏ Common Nighthawk		❏ Yellow Warbler	
Kingfisher Family		**Blackbird and Oriole Family**	
❏ Belted Kingfisher		❏ Red-winged Blackbird	
Woodpecker Family		❏ Yellow-headed Blackbird	
❏ Northern Flicker		❏ Western Meadowlark	
❏ Yellow-bellied Sapsucker		**Old World Sparrow Family**	
Lark Family		❏ House Sparrow	
❏ Horned Lark		**Finch Family**	
Swallow and Martin Family		❏ Common Redpoll	
❏ Barn Swallow		❏ Pine Grosbeak	
❏ Tree Swallow		❏ Evening Grosbeak	
❏ Cliff Swallow			

Acknowledgments

I still fondly recall my friendships with photographers Fred Lahrman, Lorne Scott, and Gary Seib. It was 1977, my first summer on the prairies, and their enthusiasm for bird photography was infectious, and we shared many memorable outings. Ranchers Francis and Myrna Walker were also an important part of my early years on the prairies. They opened their home to me, and I will always remember their warmth and generosity. In recent years, many others were generous with their help and encouragement, including Rick Martin, a biologist with Alberta's Eastern Irrigation District, ranger-in-charge John Findlay at Tillebrook & Kinbrook Island Provincial Parks, and the ranger staff at Dinosaur Provincial Park. Many researchers also took time to help me locate specific prairie birds: in the pouring rain, Shannon Haszard showed me my first American bittern nest, Robert Sissons invited me to join him and his burrowing owls and told me more about owl pellets than anyone should publicly admit, Mark Wendlandt introduced me to the charm and plight of piping plovers, and Pat Young made it possible for me to watch big-city peregrines. I owe special thanks to raptor junkie Dr. Gordon Court, who helped in many ways. I will never forget the delightful hours we spent together in blinds, and someday I will convince him that dicky-birds are more than just raptor food.

Others I would like to thank include the affable bird bander Ray Cromie, hospitable Tom and Mary Webb from Turner Valley, Wayne Wegener the wildlife trivia wizard, and the friendly folks at Calgary's Nova Photo, who always process my film with the greatest care. This is my first book with Fifth House Publishers, and I had a great time working with publisher Fraser Seely and managing editor Charlene Dobmeier. Hey, you two, let's do it again soon. Thanks also to designer John Luckhurst.

Finally, I wish to thank my wonderful wife, Aubrey Lang. She helped me with this book from the beginning, and she was always an indefatigable field partner, an enjoyable campmate, and a skilled editor and advisor. I could not have done it without her.

About the Author

In 1979, at the age of 31, Dr. Wayne Lynch left a career in emergency medicine to work full-time as a science writer and photographer. Today, he is Canada's best known and most widely published professional wildlife photographer. His photo credits include hundreds of magazine covers, thousands of calendar shots, and tens of thousands of images published in more than 30 countries. He is also the author and photographer of a dozen highly acclaimed natural history books, including: *Penguins of the World, Bears: Monarchs of the Northern Wilderness, A is for Arctic: Natural Wonders of a Polar World*, and *Married to the Wind: A Study of the Prairie Grasslands*.

© DR. GORDON COURT

His books have been described as "a magical combination of words and images."

Wayne Lynch has studied wildlife in more than 60 countries, and is a Fellow of the internationally recognized Explorers Club, headquartered in New York City. Fellows are those who have actively participated in exploration or have substantially enlarged the scope of human knowledge through scientific achievements and published reports, books, and articles. In 1997, Lynch was elected as a Fellow to the Arctic Institute of North America, in recognition of his contributions to the knowledge of polar and subpolar regions. He is also registered in Canada's *Who's Who*.